# THE CORRELATION BETWEEN PSI ENERGY AND KI

Other Books by Dr. Hiroshi Motoyama

❖ ❖ ❖

SCIENCE AND THE EVOLUTION OF CONSCIOUSNESS
Chakras, Ki and Psi

THEORIES OF THE CHAKRAS
Bridge to Higher Consciousness

TOWARD A SUPERCONSCIOUSNESS
Meditational Theory and Practice

HOW TO MEASURE AND DIAGNOSE
THE FUNCTIONS OF THE MERIDIANS AND
THE CORRESPONDING INTERNAL ORGANS

HYPNOSIS AND RELIGIOUS SUPER-CONSCIOUSNESS

# THE CORRELATION BETWEEN PSI ENERGY AND KI

Unification of Religion and Science

by Hiroshi Motoyama, Ph.D., Ph.D.

HSP

HUMAN SCIENCE PRESS
(Shukyo Shinri Shuppan)
Tokyo, Japan

---

For additional information write to:
Human Science Press
(Shukyo Shinri Shuppan)
4-11-7 Inokashira
Mitaka-shi
Tokyo 181
Japan
Tel: (0422) 48-3535
Fax: (0422) 48-3548

Published by the Human Science Press
(Shukyo Shinri Shuppan)

First edition August 1991

Cover Art: Hiroaki Kawabata
ISBN 4-87960-700-2

---

Printed in Japan

# CONTENTS

# FORWARD

The arrow of time marches us inexorably forward, away from the outmoded 'world view' of our past and towards the new world view of our near future - the next step in our collective understanding as we gradually awaken to a more complete picture of ourselves, our universe and the cosmos.

The present paradigm of science, with its four-dimensional persepctive of space-time and its four accepted forces of gravity, electromagnetism, the weak and the strong nuclear force, have shaped the thinking and technological development of this century. It has served us well and has brought great order to our scientific enterprise. However, like most world views, it is not complete and blind adherence to it limits the rate of our intellectual evolution.

For the past century, many specific examples of truly remarkable phenomena have been widely observed, carefully recorded and conscientiously investigated. These phenomena, grouped under the label "Psi-Phenomena", do not fit the tidy picture of today's accepted paradigm of science. Thus, many wish to deny its validity and acceptability and prefer to sweep the data "under the rug" rather than seriously address its possible meaning, discover ways to generate the phenomena more reproducibly than at present and expand our world picture to include this new class of subjective phenomena.

The present book by my friend, Hiroshi Motoyama, makes several important contributions to our expanding understanding: his unique experimental studies in the psi area; his connection of the energies of the acupuncture meridian system to these psi phenomena; and his design of at least two important instruments for the experimental study of these phenomena. Such instruments allow us to build important bridges between conventional areas of today's science and a future science of "subtle" energies beyond the four known and accepted today. More such instruments and even more careful experiments will allow us to also build a theoretical bridge between today's scientific paradigm and tomorrow's scientific paradigm. This will serve our evolutionary growth during the next century!

William A. Tiller, Ph. D.,
Professor, Department of Materials
Science and Engineering,
Stanford University, U.S.A.

# ACKNOWLEDGEMENTS

The Japanese original of THE CORRELATION BETWEEN PSI ENERGY AND KI — Unification of Religion and Science — was published in 1986. Although several years have passed since the publication of the Japanese original, I am truly pleased that this book is now appearing in English, and that I can share my views internationally on Psi energy and Ki, religion and science.

The manuscript was faithfully translated from the original by Ms Kiyomi Kuratani, head of the Translation Department of the Institute for Religious Psychology, and proofread/rewritten by Ms Ann Butler of the International Department of the Institute for Religious Psychology, and Dr David E. Shaner, Associate Professor of the Department of Philosophy, Furman University, U.S.A. Dr Toshiaki Harada, a former researcher at the Institute, assisted in the rewriting and made many valuable suggestions. Without the cooperation of these people, the translation of this book in English would not have been possible, and I would like to express my sincere thanks to them on this occasion. I would especially like to thank the former two staff members, who have devotedly assisted me here at the Institute for many years. Finally, I would finish the acknowledgements with my special thanks to my wife, Kaoru Motoyama, who edited the Japanese original and supervised this English edition as well.

Hiroshi Motoyama
July, 1991.

# PREFACE

For over forty years I have cultivated my inborn psychic ability through yogic practices, and have studied supernatural phenomena as a scientist holding doctoral degrees in both philosophy and physiological psychology. Over these years it has been experimentally demonstrated that Psi ability/energy, which plays an important role in the occurrence of paranormal phenomena, is closely connected to both Chakras (the energy centers taught in the yogic tradition of psi-soma medicine), and Ki and meridians (as defined in Oriental medicine).

At the same time that I was conducting scientific research on supernatural phenomena from the viewpoint of biophysics, electrophysiology, and parapsychology, I was also deepening my religious experience through yogic practices, and I realized both the truth of religion and its supernatural aspects. I came to the conclusion that religion and science do not contradict each other; rather, the world of the former underlies the latter — they are an organic unity.

Part I of this book begins with a traditional explanation of the Chakras and Nadis (of the yogic tradition) and meridians (of Oriental medicine), and the correlation between Psi energy and Ki, evidenced by the functioning of the meridians at the time when Psi energy functions as extrasensory perception or psychokinetic energy. These are discussed throughout on the basis of my personal experience of supernatural worlds and laboratory experiments. In Part II the organic unity of science and religion is discussed from its logical, experiential, and experimental view points. The mechanism of the reciprocal action of Psi energy and physical energy is also discussed in Part II.

An experiment where light was generated in a shielded room is discussed in both parts, each taking a different perspective. In Part I, this experiment is discussed in connection with the correlation among the Chakras, psychokinetic ability, and meridians. In Part II, these connections are discussed in support of the view that the religious world, where Psi energy functions, does not contradict, but underlies the world of science, which studies physical phenomena (like light) as experimental subjects. Although religion and science do not function in the same dimension, they do have a vertical relationship, indicated by different dimensions of existences, and support each other in an organic unity. While the experimental procedure indicative of their relationship is repeated in both parts, it is discussed in greater detail in Part II.

# PART I

# THE CORRELATION BETWEEN PSI ENERGY AND KI

## —Chakras, Psi Energy, Meridians and Ki—

# I. AN OVERVIEW OF YOGIC PSI-SOMA MEDICINE AND CHINESE MERIDLAN-KI MEDICINE[1]

## A. Three Bodies-Three Minds and Chakras-Nadis Taught in Yoga

### *1. Chakras and Nadis*

According to the teachings of tantric yoga, man has three bodies and three associated minds, one in each of the three major dimensions of being. During spiritual growth, a man must ascend a ladder-like progression step by step through these dimensions of being by gradually increasing his awareness of the higher realms. In this way, man can liberate himself from the limitations of the three bodies and their corresponding minds, and finally enter the highest realm of spirituality.

Specifically, the three bodies and minds are as follows:

*a.* The physical body and its mind — mind operating in association with the physical body, such as feeling and the conscious mind;

*b.* The astral (subtle) body and its mind — mind that we experience primarily as emotion;

*c.* The causal body and its mind — mind expressed as intelligence and wisdom.

Of these three, the physical body and its mind exist and work in the tangible world. This set (*a*) might be termed Yang in relation to the astral (*b*) and causal (*c*) sets which cannot be known by physical senses or thinking rooted in physical sensations. The Yang part, however, cannot be entirely separated from the other two sets because it is sustained by the hidden astral and causal Yin aspects[2].

The three body-mind sets exist and operate in different dimensions. Each set is maintained by the type of Prana (vital energy) necessary for and appropriate to its specific dimension. This distinction does not mean that these body-mind sets are separate entities, but rather that they are distinct parts of an organic whole. Each body-mind has within itself energy centers serving to control the flow of Prana as well as a system of energy channels called Nadis.

The centers which control the Nadis are known as Chakras[3]. In the physical body the channels are represented by the cardiovascular, lymphatic and acupuncture meridian systems, and the centers are represented by the brain, the nervous plexuses, and the acupuncture points. The corresponding centers and channels of all three bodies are closely interrelated.

Besides being a control center in each dimension, a Chakra works as an exchange center between the physical and the astral, and between the astral and causal dimensions. Through the Chakras, Prana in the astral body can be transformed, for instance, into energy for the physical dimension. The physical body is thereby provided with essential life energy. Yogis who have allowed themselves to be buried for incredible lengths of time and yet remained alive are examples of some of the most spectacular instances of this particular transformation. Their survival is thought to be possible due to the function of the Vishuddhi (throat) Chakra, which when activated enables a person to subsist on astral energy in the form of "Ambrosia"[4]. This energy enters the physical body by way of the Bindu Visarga of the astral body[5], and can be induced by subduing respiration with Khechari Mudra[6]. The astral energy then materializes as the oxygen, protein, fats, etc., necessary for the physical functions which enable the yogi to survive.

It is further hypothesized that the Chakras can transform physical energy into astral energy; and likewise, physical energy can be converted into psychological energy within the physical dimension.

Thus, Chakras are intermediaries for energy transfer and conversion between two proximal dimensions of being, as well as centers facilitating the energy conversion between a body and its corresponding mind.

As the Chakras are activated and awakened, man not only becomes aware of higher realms of existence, but also gains the power to enter those realms; and then, in turn, as a spiritually evolved being, it becomes possible for him to support and give life to the lower dimensions.

### 2. *Location of the Chakras and Their Functions*

There are seven Chakras. In the early stages of their awakening, the Chakras are usually perceived as either wheels of light or local auras of various colors. The locations, colors, and physical functions of the Chakras may be summarized as follows.

*Muladhara Chakra*

The Muladhara Chakra is located in the area of the coccyx. It is perceived as a wheel of red light and controls the urogenital system.

*Svadhishthana Chakra*

The Svadhishthana Chakra is located three to five centimeters below the navel. It is usually perceived as a wheel of vermilion light and controls the urogenital system.

*Manipura Chakra*

The Manipura Chakra is located around the navel. It is perceived as a wheel of blue or green light and controls the digestive system.

As an aside, it is interesting to note that in acupuncture there is an important point located at the navel called the '神闕' Shinketsu point ('神'- Divine, '闕'- void, space; CV8). This is thought to be the point where divine energy flows in and out of the body. The yoga teaching is similar to this. It claims that the Prana for the entire physical body enters from higher dimensions through the Kandasthana, a spherical region around the navel enclosing the Manipura Chakra. The Prana is then converted into physiological energy and distributed throughout the body by way of physical Nadis for the maintenance of life.

*Anahata Chakra*

The Anahata Chakra is located near the intersection of the median line and a line connecting the two nipples. Also called the Heart Chakra, it is perceived as a wheel of intense red or golden light and controls the heart. The Anahata Chakra's corresponding acupuncture point is the Danchu point (CV17) on the conception vessel meridian.

*Vishuddhi Chakra*

The Vishuddhi Chakra is located in the throat. This Chakra is perceived as a wheel of violet light and controls the respiratory organs.

*Ajna Chakra*

The Ajna Chakra is located between the eyebrows. Commonly known as the third eye, it is perceived as a wheel of white light of great intensity, as if a thousand suns were shining all at once. This Chakra controls the secretory functions of the pituitary gland as well as intellectual activities. It is said that when this Chakra is awakened, one meets one's divine self, i.e. the True Self, within oneself.

*Sahasrara Chakra*

The Sahasrara Chakra is located at the top of the head. This Chakra is in control of every aspect of the body and mind. When the Brahman Gate in this Chakra is opened, one can leave the physical body and enter the realms of the astral or causal. This Chakra is perceived as a large wheel of golden or rosy light.

The Prana absorbed at these seven Chakras is converted into the life energy of each dimension and is distributed throughout the three bodies and minds by the network of Nadis.

The minds in the astral and causal dimensions, which are not physical, are called Psi. The paranormal functioning of Psi is called Psi ability. The Prana which flows and functions in the astral and causal dimensions is called Psi energy. The essential nature of Psi ability and Psi energy functioning in the astral dimension is different from its functioning in the causal dimension. For example, control over physical energy from the causal dimension is far more cardinal than that from the astral dimension.

## B. Meridians and Ki in Oriental Medicine

There is historical evidence that the Chakra-Nadi yogic tradition was brought to China around 400-200 B.C. through Nepal and Tibet. Influenced by these traditions, it developed in China as a branch of medicine incorporating acupuncture and moxibustion.

The reason for this turn from the original traditions may be explained in the following way. Religions which originated in India (such as Buddhism, Hinduism, and Yoga) are Nirvana-oriented religions which seek the liberation of the soul or Satori (Enlightenment). This orientation is to some degree a result of environmental conditions : Deserts and semi-deserts occupy large areas of India, especially in the northwest. In places where the natural climate makes living conditions difficult life itself is a torment. The people who inhabit these regions direct their minds towards and yearn for the Other Shore and the Heavenly Kingdom. In the northwest parts of India, where the natural environment is severe, interest in the higher minds and bodies of human existence and the Other Shore is heightened.

On the other hand, in favorable environments a realistic attitude towards life, acknowledging the importance of the present, develops. China is one of these favored countries. Although there are desert and semi-desert areas along the Yellow River Valley in the west and northwest parts of China, in general the climate is mild. An attitude that affirms the present reality and seeks perpetual youth and longevity has been cultivated.

As a result, knowledge of the structure and function of higher minds and bodies in the astral and causal dimensions (Psi energy, Psi ability, Chakras, and Nadis) obtained through religious and meditative experience has been described in detail in India. Among the three minds and bodies of Indian Yoga and Hinduism, it is the mind and body which function in the physical world that have been the main concern in China. The Chakras and Nadis functioning in the physical dimension are understood in China to be the acupoints and meridians. Likewise, Prana, which flows in the meridians and nourishes the organs and tissues in the physical body, is understood as Ki.

In the next section, we will examine the meridian theory which developed in China.

### *1. Twelve Regular and Eight Independent Meridians*

The dualistic idea that the universe came from Heaven and Earth, or Yin and Yang, is characteristic of the Chinese tradition as seen in the I-Ching. Monistic ideas such as '道' (Tao), and '大極' (Taich) of Laotse, and '天' (Heaven) and '天帝' (Heavenly Lord) of Confucius influenced this Chinese tradition, and the idea that the duality of Yin and Yang originated in Taich was born. In Chinese medicine, bodily organs are divided into five Yin organs (solid organs referred to as Zang), and six Yang organs (hollow organs referred to as Fu). The meridians which distribute Ki (vital force) to these five Yin and six Yang organs are classified as the six Yin and six Yang meridians.

*Five Yin and Six Yang Organs*

The five Yin organs are the lung, heart, liver, spleen, and kidney. The six Yang organs are the stomach, gall bladder, small intestine, large intestine, urinary bladder, and triple heater[7].

*Twelve Regular Meridians*

The following is a diagram of the relation among the twelve regular meridians (six meridian pairs of the Yin-Yang relationship) and the three Yin-Yang channels. Each of the Yin-Yang meridians (which are paired by connective lines) form a Yin-Yang pair in the Yin-Yang relationship.

MERIDIANS

| 3 Yin Channels | Yin | | Yang | 3 Yang Channels |
|---|---|---|---|---|
| Greater Yin | (ARM) Lung | → | Large Intestine (ARM) | Sun Bright |
| | (LEG) Spleen | ← | Stomach (LEG) | |
| Lesser Yin | (ARM) Heart | → | Small Intestine (ARM) | Greater Yang |
| | (LEG) Kidney | ← | Urinary Bladder (LEG) | |
| Absolute Yin | Heart Constrictor (ARM) | → | Triple Heater (ARM) | Lesser Yang |
| | (LEG) Liver | ← | Gall Bladder (LEG) | |

**Table I − 1**: Twelve Meridians, Flow of Ki, Yin-Yang Relationship & 3 Yin-Yang Channels

*Eight Independent Channels*

| *Yin Channels* | *Yang Channels* |
|---|---|
| Ren Channel | Du Channel |
| Dai Channel | Ching Channel |
| Yinqiao Channel | Yangiao Channel |
| Yinwei Channel | Yangwei Channel |

### 2. *Organs/Tissues and Meridians*

The table below indicates the correlation between organs/

tissues and meridians. The information it contains is based upon teachings from acupuncture classics, my own clinical experience (as well as that of acupuncturists throughout the history of the practice), and finally electrophysiological measurements of meridian functions performed at the Institute for Religious Psychology.

| ORGANS／TISSUES | MERIDIANS |
|---|---|
| Urogenital System (kidney, urinary bladder, urinary tract, uterus, ovary, prostate gland) | Kidney, Urinary Bladder, Small Intestine, Triple Heater & Liver meridians |
| Digestive System (liver, gall bladder, stomach, large intestine, small intestine, pancreas) | Liver, Gall Bladder Spleen, Stomach, Large Intestine & Small Intestine meridians |
| Circulatory System (heart, arteries, veins) | Heart, Heart Constrictor & Small Intestine meridians |
| Respiratory System (lung, bronchus) | Lung, Heart Constrictor & Large Intestine meridians |
| Skin | Lung & Large Intestine meridians |
| Muscle | Liver & Gall Bladder meridians |
| Central Nervous System | Urinary Bladder, Small Intestine, Governor Vessel & Conception Vessel meridians |
| Bone | Kidney meridian |
| Whole Body | Heart Constrictor & Triple Heater meridians |

**Table I − 2**

### 3. *Chakras, Organs and Meridians*

As previously explained in the section 'Three Bodies-

Three Minds of Yoga and Chakras-Nadis Taught in Yoga', there is a correlation between specific organs/tissues and Chakras. The table below is a compilation of the correlation between specific organs/tissues and Chakras, and that between organs/ tissues and meridians.

| CHAKRAS | ORGANS/TISSUES | MERIDIANS |
|---|---|---|
| Muladhara & Svadhishthana | Urogenital System | Kidney, Urinary Bladder, Small Intestine, Liver & Triple Heater |
| Manipura | Digestive System | Liver, Gall Bladder, Stomach, Spleen, Large Intestine & Small Intestine |
| Anahata | Circulatory System | Heart, Heart Constrictor & Small Intestine |
| Vishuddhi | Respiratory System | Lung, Heart Constrictor & Large Intestine |
| Ajna & Sahasrara | Central Nervous System | Urinary Bladder, Small Intestine, Governor Vessel & Conception Vessel |

**Table I – 3**

The meridians, which differ from the nervous system, begin and end near the tips of the toes and fingers. They flow longitudinally in the body, passing and distributing Ki to various organs and tissues. Thus, one meridian correlates with several organs/tissues.

### 4. *Chakras and Psi Ability*

The following table shows the correspondence between the nature of Psi ability and the Chakra to which it belongs. It was compiled both through a survey of the descriptions of the Chakras by those who had awakened them, and from my own research and experience.

From this study, it can be concluded that there is a close

| CHAKRAS | PSI ABILITY |
|---|---|
| Muladhara & Svadhishthana | Spontaneous & unconscious PK & ESP ability |
| Manipura | Mainly ESP ability with awareness |
| Anahata | Mainly PK ability with awareness |
| Vishuddhi | Ability for purification of mind & body |
| Ajna | Far more fundamental PK & ESP ability |
| Sahasrara | Liberation from the restraints of the physical body: for example, astral projection in its lower dimensional awakening |

**Table I − 4**

connection among meridians, Chakras, and Psi ability obtained through religious experience. As another example of this connection, the correspondence between the Chakras and acupoints is given as Figure I-1.

In the following chapters, experiments conducted at the Institute for Religious Psychology will be discussed. These experiments were performed in order to investigate whether or not Psi ability developed through religious practice actually exists; and if so, whether or not there exists the above hypothesized connection.

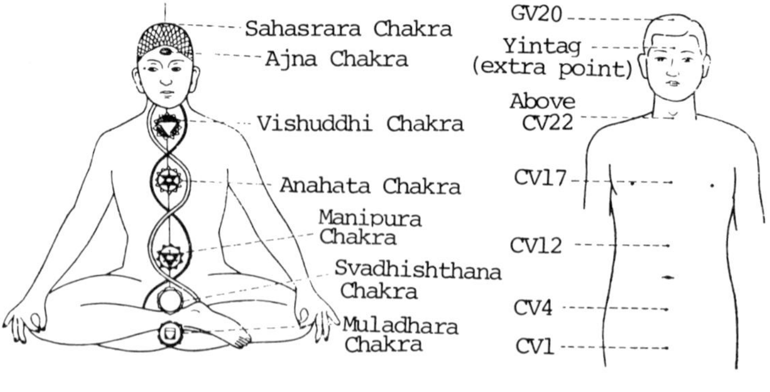

| CHAKRAS | LOCATION | CORRESPONDING ACUPOINTS | SECRETING GLANDS & PLEXUSES |
|---|---|---|---|
| Sahasrara Chakra | Top of the head | GV20 | Cerebral cortex |
| Ajna Chakra | Between the eyebrows | Yintang (extra point) | Pituitary & Pineal glands, Hypothalamus |
| Vishuddhi Chakra | Throat | Above CV22 | Thyroid gland |
| Anahata Chakra | Heart | CV17 | Cardiac plexus |
| Manipura Chakra | Stomach | CV12 | Solar plexus |
| Svadhishthana Chakra | Below the navel | CV4 | Lumbosacral plexus |
| Muladhara Chakra | Coccyx | CV1 | Coccygeal plexus |

**Figure I-1:** Location of Chakras and Corresponding Acupoints

Notes for Chapter I

1) *Acupuncture Meridian System*: In the acupuncture theory developed in China, Ki or vital force is considered to circulate in the human body through a systematic net work of energy channels. These channels are usually referred to as "meridians". (Translator's note — hereafter 'tr.')

2) *Yin and Yang*: A philosophical concept used in traditional Chinese medicine. According to this concept, there are two fundamental principles or forces in the universe called Yin and Yang, opposing and complementing each other. Yang is seen as hot, male, heaven, light, active, exterior, while Yin is associated with cold, female, earth, dark, passive, interior. All aspects and phenomena in the natural world and in human beings can exist through the interactions of these forces. When there is a balance between these two principles, there is harmony and health. When there is imbalance, there is disharmony and disease. (tr.)

3) *Chakras*: "Chakra" is the Sanskrit word that means "wheel of light". In the art of many religions, a wheel of light is drawn around the head of saints and divine beings. This is one indication of how the Chakras have been perceived. Yoga teaches that the life energy of the astral and causal dimensions starts active functioning, when the practitioner can break through the physical functioning of the body and mind,

that is, the way of his physical being, through deep meditation, and can leap into the astral and causal dimensions through mental growth. In this state, his Chakras start to shine with a specific light and Psi abilities will be obtained. This has been experienced by practitioners of many religions.

4) *Ambrosia* : Divine nectar which rejuvenates the body.

5) *Bindu Visarga* : A minor center which is in a close relationship with the Vishuddhi Chakra. According to yogic tradition, the physical location of the Bindu Visarga is said to be near the top of the brain, towards the back of the head. There is a very slight depression or pit there, which contains a small amount of a liquid secretion. Within this pit there is a slight elevation, and this is the exact location of the Bindu. Bindu means drop or 'spot' and Bindu Visarga is said to be the 'seat of divine nectar' in yogic tradition. It is said that it is possible for one to maintain the physical body by creating the energy and materials of the physiological dimension within one's own body; and that physical longevity and immortality is possible when the Vishuddhi Chakra is awakened and this nectar is purified in the same Chakra.

6) *Khechari Mudra* : Mudras are not merely physical postures, but practices which generate a strong psychic effect upon the beings of a student, facilitating spiritual advancement. Khechari Mudra is the Mudra in which the mouth is closed and the tongue is rolled backwards so that the underside of the tongue touches the back of the palate. This Mudra helps the student awaken the Kundalini Shakti and also preserves the vital energy in the body. It is one of the very important Mudras of yogic practices. (tr.)

7) *Triple Heater Meridian* : Western medicine recognizes no equivalent to the triple heater (三焦). '三' means three or triple and '焦' refers to energy or Ki. Ki is divided into three parts in the body : upper energy controlling the body from the diaphragm upwards ; middle energy which regulates the digestive organs; and lower energy in control of the lower part of the body. (tr.)

---

# II. PSI EXPERIMENT
## —Generation of Light—

### A. AMI Data of a Psychic

The subject of the AMI data (old model; Figure Ⅱ-1)[1] is M.Y., a 29-year-old American female, with inborn psychic abilities. The results of this experiment indicate a wider than normal range of activity between the left (L%) and right (R%) branches of the heart and heart constrictor meridians[2]. These meridians have a close connection with the Anahata Chakra (the Psi energy center connected to the heart) and the occurrence of PK phenomena (PK - Psychokinesis : movement of physical objects by the mind without the use of physical means). The wide range of meridian activity detected suggests the activation of the Anahata Chakra in this subject.

A similar abnormal tendency (wider range of function) is observed in the meridians connected to the Manipura Chakra (the center closely aligned with the digestive system, emotions, and ESP ability); that is, the spleen, stomach and stomach branch meridians. Furthermore, an abnormality is also found in the function of the urinary bladder and small intestine meridians connected to the Svadhishthana Chakra (the center in charge of control of the urogenital

Date June 24, 1977 PM 4:15

0.5 V 21 T(°C) 996 mb 70 %

No.

Name M. Y. M (F)

age

Birth Date

History of disease

Chief complaint, Subjective symptoms

Blood presure

Diagnosis, Treatment

| | | |
|---|---|---|
| $\bar{X}$ of Li, Ri | BP | 134.253 |
| | AP | 2.948 |
| | P | 131.305 |
| $\bar{D}$ of difference / $\bar{X}$ of Li, Ri | BP | -0.316 |
| | AP | 0.375 |
| | P | -0.319 |
| σ of L%, R% | BP | -0.327 |
| | AP | 0.379 |
| | P | -0.330 |

----- Lenient —— Rigid
(Criteria for overactive, deteriorated & unstable functioning)

L%, R%:

| | Deteriorated | | Normal | Overactive | |
|---|---|---|---|---|---|
| BP.P | 0.78 | 0.85 | | 1.11 | 1.21 |
| AP | 0.49 | 0.60 | | 1.21 | 1.59 |

D%:

| | Stable | | Unstable |
|---|---|---|---|
| BP.P | 0.00 | 1.21 | 1.80 |
| AP | 0.00 | 1.21 | 1.90 |

$\bar{D}/\bar{X}$:

| | Deviated | Normal | Unstable |
|---|---|---|---|
| BP.P | 0.08 | | 0.15 |
| AP | 0.22 | | 0.66 |

σ of L%, R%:

| | Deviated and constricted functioning of all the meridians | Stable | Unstable functioning |
|---|---|---|---|
| BP.P | 0.10 | | 0.26 |
| AP | 0.21 | | 0.71 |

| meridian | | D% | L% | R% | (L%+R%)/2 |
|---|---|---|---|---|---|
| Lung | BP | 0.423 | 0.945 | 1.079 | 1.012 |
| | AP | 0.817 | 1.355 | 1.050 | 1.203 |
| | P | 0.450 | 0.936 | 1.080 | 1.008 |
| Large Intestine | BP | 0.120 | 0.766 | 0.804 | 0.785 |
| | AP | 0.182 | 0.915 | 0.847 | 0.881 |
| | P | 0.126 | 0.763 | 0.803 | 0.783 |
| Heart Constrictor | BP | 1.645 | -1.250 | -0.729 | 0.989 |
| | AP | -2.908 | 1.491 | -0.406 | 0.949 |
| | P | 1.590 | -1.245 | -0.736 | 0.990 |
| Diaphragm | BP | 0.000 | -0.722 | -0.722 | -0.722 |
| | AP | 0.908 | 1.152 | 0.813 | 0.983 |
| | P | 0.023 | -0.712 | -0.720 | -0.716 |
| Triple Heater | BP | 0.754 | -0.632 | 0.871 | -0.751 |
| | AP | 0.182 | 1.152 | 1.084 | 1.118 |
| | P | 0.769 | -0.620 | 0.866 | -0.743 |
| Heart | BP | 0.941 | 1.027 | -0.729 | 0.878 |
| | AP | -2.091 | 1.491 | 0.711 | 1.101 |
| | P | 0.898 | 1.017 | -0.729 | 0.873 |
| Small Intestine | BP | 0.518 | -0.528 | -0.692 | -0.610 |
| | AP | 0.273 | 0.847 | 0.949 | 0.898 |
| | P | 0.517 | -0.521 | -0.686 | -0.603 |
| Spleen | BP | -3.196 | -2.122 | 1.109 | -1.615 |
| | AP | -3.364 | -1.933 | 0.677 | 1.305 |
| | P | -3.148 | -2.126 | 1.119 | -1.622 |
| Liver | BP | 0.445 | 0.908 | 1.049 | 0.978 |
| | AP | 0.638 | 0.983 | 0.745 | 0.864 |
| | P | 0.467 | 0.906 | 1.056 | 0.981 |
| Stomach | BP | -1.999 | 0.952 | -1.585 | -1.269 |
| | AP | 1.000 | 1.389 | -1.763 | 1.576 |
| | P | -1.998 | 0.942 | -1.581 | -1.262 |
| Stomach Blanch | BP | -2.305 | 0.863 | -1.593 | -1.228 |
| | AP | 0.544 | 1.152 | 1.355 | 1.254 |
| | P | -2.320 | 0.856 | -1.599 | -1.228 |
| Gall Bladder | BP | 0.306 | 1.094 | 0.997 | 1.406 |
| | AP | 0.182 | 0.644 | 0.576 | 0.610 |
| | P | 0.305 | 1.104 | 1.006 | 1.055 |
| Kidney | BP | 0.799 | 1.198 | 0.945 | 1.072 |
| | AP | 0.088 | 0.644 | 0.677 | 0.660 |
| | P | 0.811 | 1.211 | 0.951 | 1.081 |
| Urinary Bladder | BP | 0.543 | 0.952 | 1.124 | 1.038 |
| | AP | 0.817 | 0.745 | -0.440 | 0.592 |
| | P | 0.571 | 0.957 | 1.139 | 1.048 |

| Li, Ri | | |
|---|---|---|
| 0. | 126.933 | 39.972 |
| 1. | 144.932 | 30.975 |
| 2. | 102.889 | 26.992 |
| 3. | 107.994 | 24.986 |
| 4. | 167.901 | 43.984 |
| 5. | 97.920 | 11.977 |
| 6. | 96.979 | 33.984 |
| 7. | 96.979 | 23.983 |
| 8. | 84.890 | 33.984 |
| 9. | 116.993 | 31.978 |
| 10. | 137.947 | 43.984 |
| 11. | 97.920 | 20.974 |
| 12. | 70.921 | 24.986 |
| 13. | 92.950 | 27.995 |
| | 133.918 | 16.992 |
| 24. | 160.916 | 18.998 |
| 25. | 126.933 | 19.971 |
| 26. | 127.873 | 21.977 |
| 27. | 150.976 | 12.980 |

**Figure II - 1**: AMI Data of M.Y.

system). Although the facts suggest that these Chakras were activated in this subject, the information we obtained was not sufficient to conclusively make this determination. The following experiment was therefore conducted with the

Chakra Instrument.

## B. A Test of Psychic Ability with M.Y. (Generation of Light)

### 1. *Experimental Set-up and Test Methods*

The room in which this test was conducted is divided into the experiment room itself as well as a shielded room (160 cm × 220 cm in size) which was constructed in one corner of the experiment room (Figure II-2).

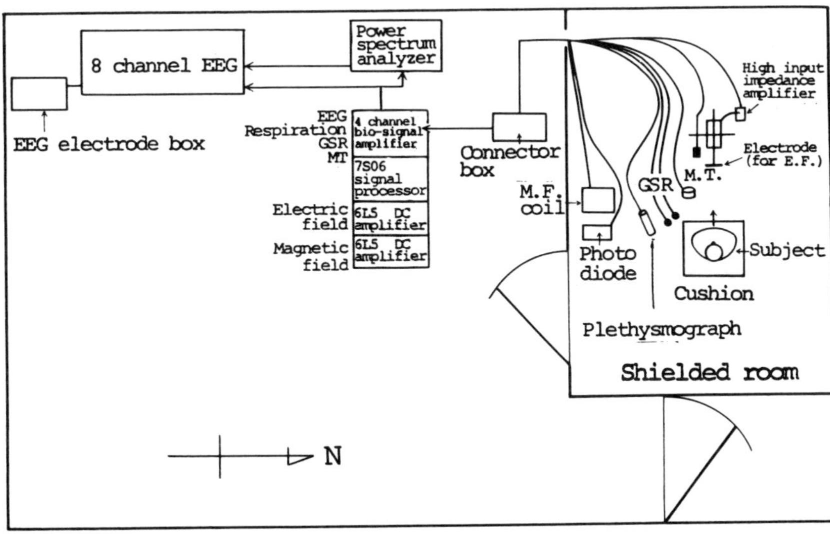


**Figure II - 2**: Experimental Set-up

The six walls of this shielded room are constructed of copper plate (.4 mm), lead plate (5 mm) and concrete. Thus, the space inside is completely isolated from physical energy disturbances (electricity, X-rays, light, radio waves, sound, etc.), but not from earth magnetism. A system referred to as the Chakra Instrument is installed in this shielded room. This instrument was designed to record the subtle changes in the energy fields surrounding the human body, and to investigate Psi energy conversion into physical energy as a product of the activity of the energy centers. The Chakra Instrument System consists of 1) an instrument which is able to monitor static biopotential without attaching electrodes to the subject, 2) an instrument to monitor the magnetic field, 3) a photoelectric cell sensitive to a wide diapason of light frequencies, and 4) biomedical sensors and amplifiers needed to monitor the rate of the subject's respiration, plethysmograph, minor tremor (MT)[3] and GSR (Galvanic Skin Response) (Figure Ⅱ-3).

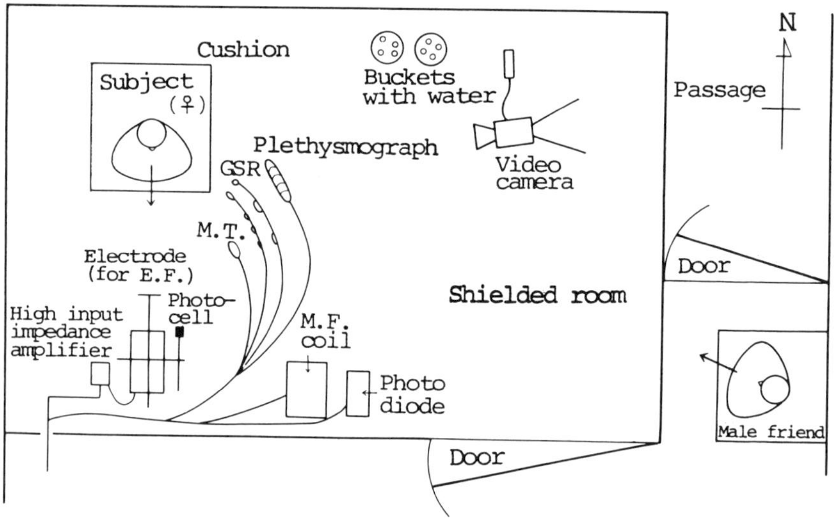


**Figure Ⅱ - 3**: Experimental Set-up in the Shielded Room

Subtle changes occurring within the shielded room are detected by these transducers and instruments, then passed to outside amplifiers, and finally are noted on the strip chart recorder.

The non-contact disk electrode is placed about thirty centimeters from the subject and wired directly to an amplifier (input impedance 1000 mega-ohm, made of an FET) sensitive to subtle changes in the room. Given that the impedance of the usual electroencephalograph is 10-20 mega-ohm, it should be easy to imagine the sensitivity of this amplifier. In measurements of small changes in weak electric fields, non-contact electrodes must be used. Lack of contact is important because the potential change resulting from polarization of the electrode paste (occurring when the electrodes are attached on the body surface) is larger than the potential changes in such weak electric fields. The MF coil (which detects magnetic field fluctuations) and the photoelectric cell (light) are installed to the left-front of the subject in order to detect fluctuations in the earth's magnetic field and any light which may result from the conversion of Psi energy during the subject's concentration.

Although this may digress from the explanation of the light experiment, the living organism has static biopotential on its surface. We found, using this instrument, the potential on the back of the body to be two to five times higher than that on the front. For example, if it is about 600 V on the back, then it will be 200 V on the front. This information would seem to support the acupuncture classics' teachings that Ki enters into the organs through the associated points on the back of the body, and gathers in the alarm points on the front of the body[4].

In the set-up for this experiment, the subject was seated on a cushion in the shielded room with a video camera placed to her left. While concentrating on the Ajna Chakra, she tried to psychically generate light.

### 2. *Polygraph Recording*

When the door was opened before the subject started any concentration, the photoelectric cell recorded mountain-like waves due to the light entering the shielded room (Figure II-4). However, the recording of the light generation during the subject's concentration period (Psi energy conversion into light) was completely different from the mountain-like ones recorded previously (Figure II-5). It was brief and the wave forms were sharp.

The video camera also recorded light generation during

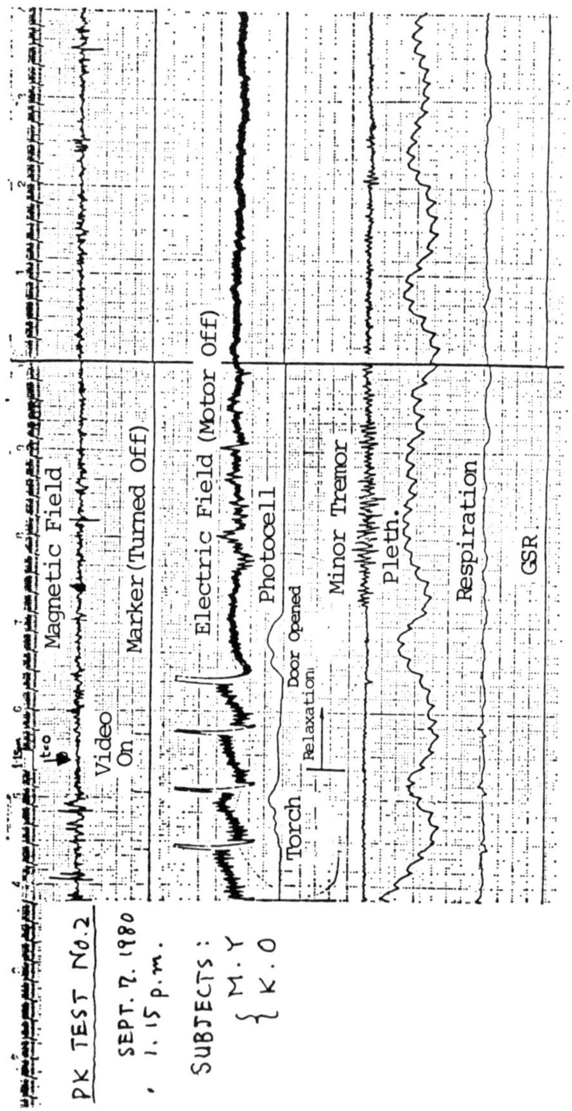


**Figure II - 4 :** Polygraph — Torch light & when the door was opened

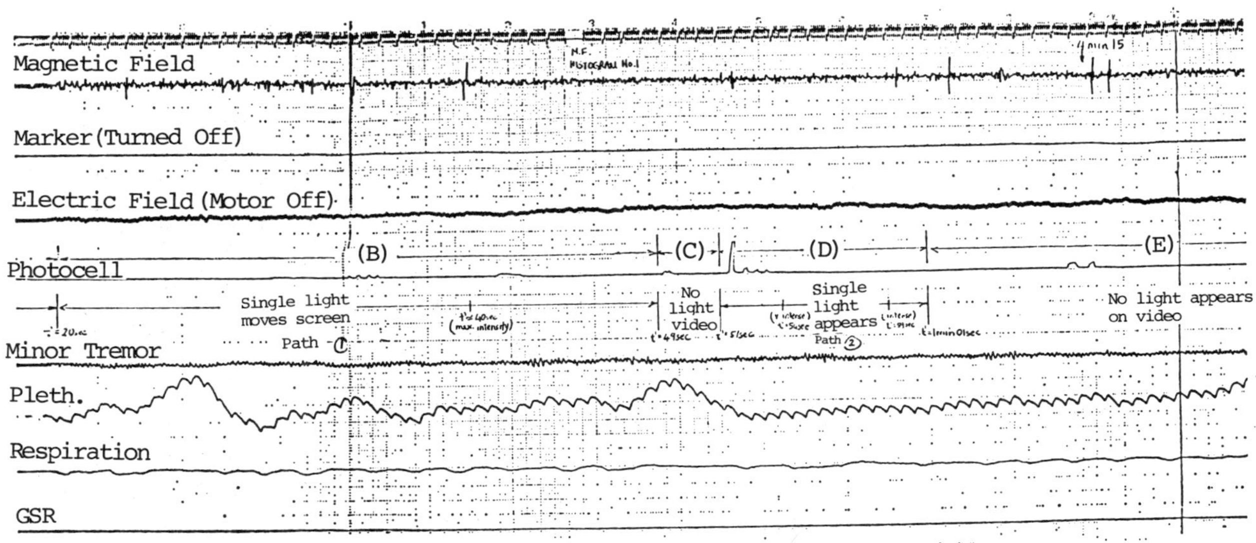


**Figure II - 5**: Polygraph — During concentration and meditation

the period of concentration. In the film, light was recorded moving vertically and/or horizontally, becoming brighter, dimmer, or disappearing at times between the eyebrows and in the vicinity of the subject's navel and chest. Although the video camera's field of view did not allow recording lower than the navel, the light seems to have originated in the area of the Svadhishthana Chakra in the lower abdomen.

In previous research on psychokinetic phenomena, the following physical conditions have been commonly observed while psychokinetic powers were functioning and Psi energy was being converted into physical energy (such as light, other electricity, or magnetism): Respiration is suspended for several seconds or more, and excitation of the sympathetic nervous system is indicated by frequent recording of GSR signals, especially with symptoms of strong excitation in the cardiovascular system. In this recording, however, the amplitudes of respiration, GSR, and MT were low, and were not clearly recorded. These recordings indicate that the subject was relaxed throughout these segments[5].

A specific feature common to those with Psi ability is an unusually wide range of functioning of the autonomic nervous system. Among those with Psi ability, those who are more competent in PK ability have a notably wider functional range in the autonomic nervous branches which control the cardiovascular system. This increased range is indicated by rhythmical fluctuations of the baselines of the plethysmograph. In contrast, the baselines of ordinary subjects are recorded as being nearly flat. This fluctuation shows that the peripheral blood volume in the hand changes rhythmically in the former, although it is constant and unchanging in the latter. Such rhythmical fluctuation of the base line was also monitored in our subject (Figure Ⅱ-5).

The data taken during the period of the subject's concentration does not reflect significant changes in the electric field, but does reveal small fluctuations in the magnetic field. When magnetic fluctuations occur it is apparent that the subject held her breath. It seems that Psi energy conversion generally occurs when the body has a dynamic balance with tonus in both the sympathetic and parasympathetic nervous systems, and with the breath held. At this time, the meridian is likely to be considerably excited, although the meridian function was not monitored in this experiment[6].

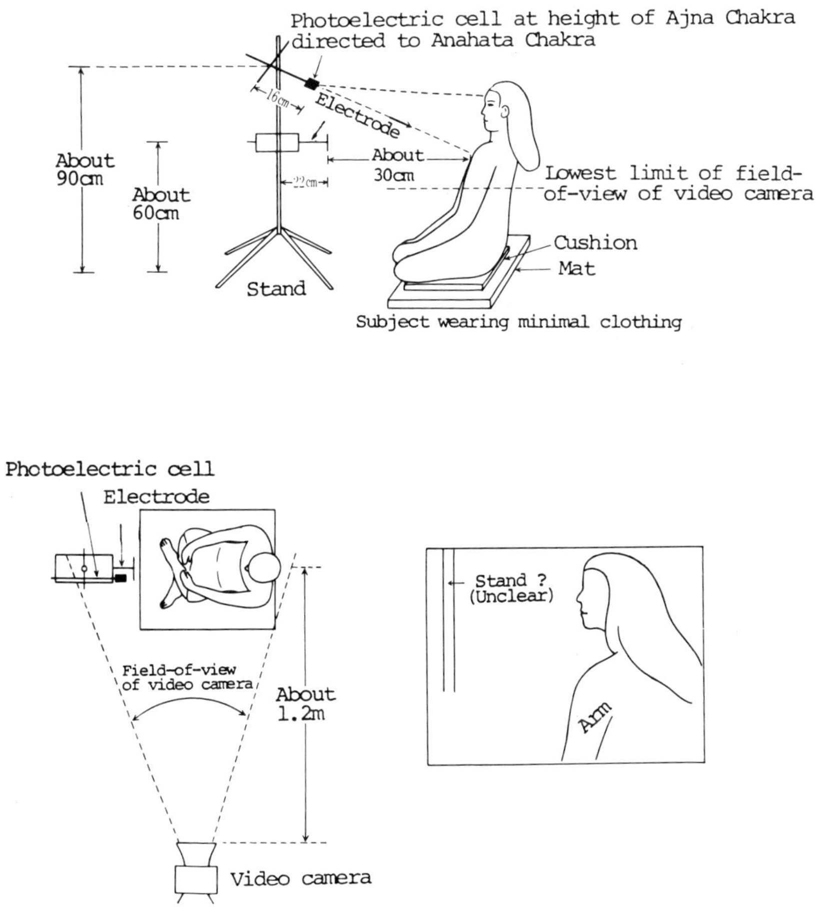


**Figure II - 6**: Location and Field-of-View of the Photoelectric Cell and Video Camera

## C. Implications of the Light Experiment

### 1. *Christian Interpretation of Miracles is Denied*

Christian doctrine explains that miracles occur when God, as the supreme or first cause, intercedes into the domain of the subordinate physical world, thus breaking the causal nexus described by so-called natural laws[7]. This idea originates in Tertullian's dictum 'Credo Quia Impossible', taught in the Age of the Fathers, one to two hundred years after the death of Jesus Christ. However, I think that the light experiment refutes this Christian interpretation of miracles, and I will explain my reasons.

The video camera was placed about 1.2 meters to the left of the subject and the photoelectric cell about 30 cm front and left of the subject. Although both the instruments recorded light generation (Psi energy conversion into light), in some cases the photoelectric cell caught the light and the video camera did not 〔segment (E) in Figure Ⅱ-5〕. The extent of light detection or recording differs between the two instruments, for example the video camera might not have recorded the light's movement away from the field of vision of the lens (Figure Ⅱ-6). This fact suggests that even Psi or mental energy follows natural laws when it is converted into physical energy. This suggestion may allow changes in the Christian concept of miracles, and may put an end to the dispute which has continued for over one thousand years, between religion and science on such matters.

### 2. *Subjective and Objective Science*

At present, science is based on the law of energy conservation. However, if we can suppose that Psi or mental energy is converted into physical energy (as seen in the previously mentioned experiment) it is not impossible to suppose that natural energy may be constantly changing in a manner more subtle than the capacity of our instruments permits us to detect. Conceivably, it only appears that energy is conserved and does not vanish. Here arises the potential to replace this paradigm of natural science (the law of energy conservation). It also occasions the consideration of science from a completely different viewpoint.

Scientists today neglect consideration of the mental functioning of those involved in research and experimentation. In psychokinetic light generation, however, light will not be produced if it is not so willed. That is, the phenomenon itself is the same as the natural production of light (which is commonly seen in the physical world), but its psychokinetic production depends on the will of the subject. This relationship means that the phenomenon itself is subjective. Once converted into light, the light phenomenon follows natural laws and is objective; but the generation of light is caused by the subjective will of the mind and Psi energy. Therefore, physical phenomena may actually be both objective and subjective.

## D. Conclusion of Chapter II

Based on the light experiment and measurements of the subject's meridian functions, it can be surmised that the Psi ability which generated PK phenomena is closely related to the heart and heart constrictor meridians, which are closely related to the Anahata Chakra; stomach and spleen meridians, which in turn share a close connection with the Manipura Chakra; and the kidney, urinary bladder and small intestine meridians, which have a close relationship with the Svadhishthana Chakra.

After the experiment, the video tape was examined carefully. The area of light generation was recorded below the navel (the physical location of the Svadhishthana Chakra) and appeared several centimeters away from the body. It is therefore possible that Psi energy was spontaneously rather than consciously converted into light energy through the Svadhishthana Chakra.

There is another mechanism for light generation which

can be assumed : The Psi energy, emitted or functioning through the Svadhishthana Chakra, caused a transition of the outer-orbit electrons of certain atoms in the shielded room into the inner orbits of those atoms, thereby releasing light energy. In this case, the Psi energy changed the movement of matter, and this movement released physical energy, rather than Psi energy being converted into light energy of the physical dimension. Whether it is correct to state that Psi energy was converted into physical energy, or to state that the Psi energy influenced the movement of matter resulting in energy change, cannot be determined at the present stage. Further studies should reveal more on this subject.

Even at this early stage, however, the following can be said: When a certain degree of evolved consciousness has been attained, and the mind or spirit enters, even partially, into a state freed from physical restrictions, the Chakras become active in dimensions higher than the astral. As a result, Psi ability starts to function. The close relationship among Psi ability, Psi energy and Chakras has long been empirically known. Observing meridian measurements with the AMI in those subjects with activated/awakened Chakras has made it clear that Chakra activation/awakening generates a marked functional change in the meridians which are in close relationship with that specific Chakra.

Furthermore, by utilizing the Chakra Instrument it became possible to demonstrate whether or not the Chakra is truly awakened by examining whether Psi phenomena are generated by Psi ability, which is said to have a close connnection with the supposed activation/awakening of the Chakras.

In this chapter the light experiment and its implications concerning PK ability (which produces changes in physical energy and movement of matter) have been discussed. In the next chapter the results of an experiment on ESP ability, that enables one to know both what cannot be seen with ordinary senses and what is in others' minds, will be discussed.

## Notes for Chapter II

1) *The AMI*: An acronym for the Apparatus for measuring the functioning of the Meridians and their corresponding Internal organs. The active electrodes of the AMI are attached to the Sei point of each meridian. Indifferent electrodes are attached to the forearms. 3.0 Volt ; 1 $\mu$ sec wave pulses are then sequentially applied between the active and indifferent electrode pairs.

The AMI monitors:

*a*) BP (Before Polarization) current value : This is the value of the current which flows before the generation of polarization at the outer and inner sides of the epidermal barrier membranes (one of the homeostatic abilities of the organism), and is the parameter established for the meridian function of the organism.

*b*) AP (After Polarization) current value : This is the value of the current which flows after the generation of polarization. This value is the parameter of the autonomic nervous function of the organism.

*c*) IQ (Integrated Polarization Charge) : This measures the total electrical charge which accumulates at the conclusion of the polarization against the externally applied potential, and is the parameter of the metabolic function of the organism.

*d*) TC (Time Constant) : This measures the time necessary for the above-mentioned polarization to be completed.

The AMI monitors the above four parameters while its external computer system analyzes them according to the following:

*e*) L%, R% : The values obtained by dividing the value obtained at each Sei point with the average of 28 Sei point values, that is, left-right Sei point values of the fourteen meridians, respectively, for the BP, AP, IQ, and TC parameters. The left side relative value is represented by L % and the right side relative value by R%. — Together with the traditional twelve regular meridians from the lung to the liver, the stomach branch meridian is monitored near the lateral base of the third toenail. In the

AMI measurement the diaphragm meridian is also monitored near the ulnar base of the third fingernail. (tr.) —

*f* ) D % : The value obtained by dividing Di (difference between left-right Sei point values of the bilateral branches of each of the fourteen meridians) with $\bar{D}$ (the average of left-right differences of the fourteen meridians) for each of the BP, AP, IQ, and TC parameters.

*g* ) AVE : The average of all the values obtained at 28 Sei points for each of the BP, AP, TC, and IQ parameters.

*h* ) SD : Standard Deviation of the values obtained at 28 Sei points for each of the BP, AP. TC and IQ parameters.

*i* ) F/T: The ratio between the average of fourteen finger Sei point values and that of fourteen toe Sei point values for each of the BP, AP. TC and IQ parameters.

*j* ) L/R : The ratio between the average of the left fourteen Sei point values and of the right fourteen Sei point values for each of the BP, AP, TC and IQ parameters.

After computer analysis, the computer prints out the values with the indication 'normal' or ' abnormal' according to the normal-abnormal criteria. On the basis of the above data, the computer also prints out:

*k* ) The present condition of the meridian function and bodily health, as well as the stage of disease, if any.

*l* ) The acupuncture points to be treated by needles and other means on the basis of the symptom complex as mentioned in *k*).

*m*) The active/inactive condition of astral energy centers (Chakras) reflected by the functional condition of the meridians.

*n* ) The constitution and character surmised in relation to *k*) and *m*).

For details of the AMI system and its data assessments, please refer to:

*i* ) Motoyama, H., *How to Measure and Diagnose the Functions of the Meridians and their Corresponding Internal Organs*, The Institute for Religious Psychology, Tokyo, 1975.

*ii* ) Motoyama, H., "Electrophysiological and Preliminary Biochemical Studies of Skin Properties in Relation to the Acupuncture Meridian", *Research for Religion and Parapsychology*, June, 1980, pp. 1-37.

*iii*) Motoyama, H., "A Biophysical Elucidation of the Meridian and Ki Energy", *Research for Religion and Parapsychology*, August, 1981.

*iv*) Motoyama, H., " Meridians and Ki ", *Research for Religion and Parapsychology*, December, 1986.

2) *Wider than Normal Range of Activity*: The activity imbalance of L % and R % is very large as represented by D % in note 1)-*f*).

3) *MT*: Micro-vibration of the Skin Surface. (tr.)

4) *Associated and Alarm Points*: The associated points of each meridian are located bilaterally on the back of the body; and alarm points are located on the front of the body. Both have a close Yin-Yang relationship. Both associated and alarm points clearly indicate the condition of the meridian/nervous function and/or the internal organs, and are used in diagnoses and treatment. (tr.)

5) *These recordings show the subject was relaxed throughout these segments*: In the data taken in July, 1980, the gain in GSR signals and respiration was low, and the changes during the concentration were not clearly recorded. As a reference, a chart in which a clearly recorded change in GSR signals and respiration is given here as Figures II-7 and 8.

Figures II-7 and 8 were obtained in an experiment conducted in February, 1979, with the cooperation of the same subject, M.Y. The frequency components of the magnetic field fluctuations were analyzed in terms of an internal histogram, with the threshold set as zero volts, taken by a signal processor. After a pre-set number of samplings had been completed, the signal processor printed out the histogram pattern. During the subject's concentration period (Figure II-8), a marked narrowing and division (two sharp peaks) of the frequency range were recorded. Neither of these results are normally detected in natural fluctuations of earth magnet-

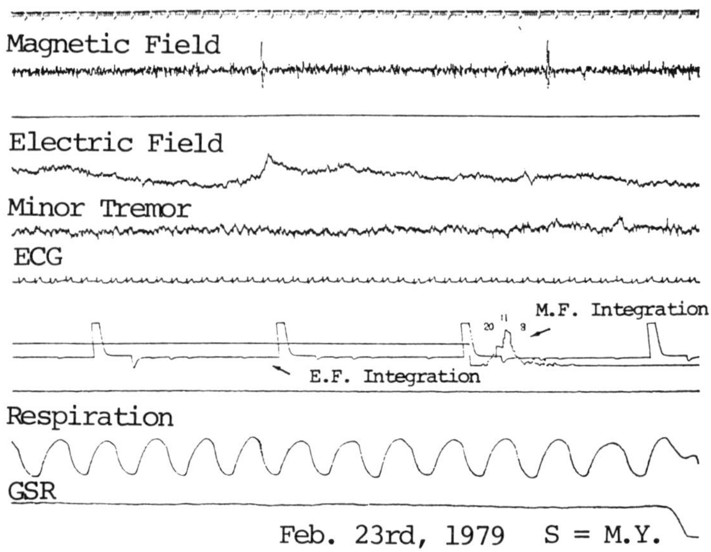


**Figure II - 7** : Before Concentration on the Ajna Chakra (Subject : M.Y.)

ism and were not recorded before the concentration period (Figure II-7). At the same time, changes in GSR signals and respiration were clearly recorded in this chart.

When Psi energy is converted in physical energy, it is sometimes converted into light, sometimes into electrical energy, sometimes into magnetic energy, and at other times into an anti-gravitational force resulting in the ability to levitate heavy materials. It is rare that Psi energy is converted into all energy forms at once; more typically, it is converted into one of the above-mentioned energy forms.

6) A more detailed explanation on this experiment is found in Part II of this book, "Towards the Unification of Science and Religion". (tr.)

7) *Supreme and Subordinate Cause* : " Thomas Aquinas (1225-1274) has been the dominant influence on Christian theology since the Middle Ages. He explained the existence of miracles in the following manner : When a thing comes into being, it

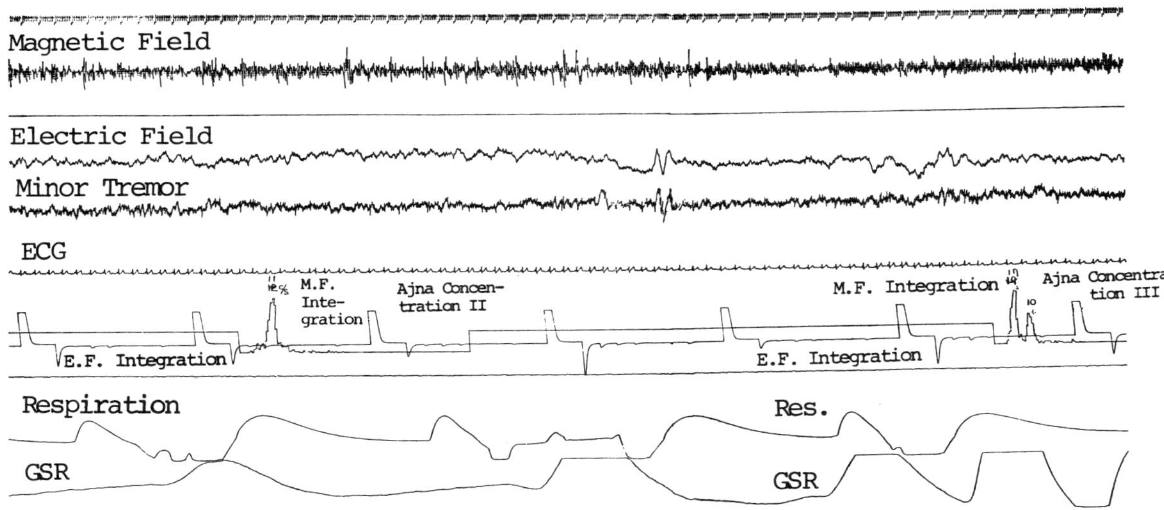


**Notes:**

**Ajna Concentration II:**

The frequency range of the M.F. was 7Hz(min) to 25Hz(max) with a sharp peak at 11Hz. The signals recorded were mostly in the range from 9Hz to 14Hz.

**Ajna Concentration III:**

The frequency range split into portions with two sharp peaks, one ranging from 12Hz(min) to 30 Hz(max) with a peak at 17Hz, and the other ranging from 8Hz(min) to 11Hz(max) with a peak at 10Hz.

**Figure II - 8**: During Concentration on the Ajna Chakra

is due to the supreme will of God. Following this will there are subordinate causes, such as nature and reason, which work harmoniously together to produce material things and natural phenomena. As a result, houses are built, people speak, objects fall, electricity sparks, and so on. These phenomena are caused by God's power working in harmony with the laws of nature, which are themselves a result of God's supreme will. Thus, it can be said that all phenomena are the indirect result of God's supreme will. However, upon occasion earnest prayer may create a situation in which the supreme will supersedes subordinate causes, and a phenomenon occurs which seems to violate the conventional rules of nature. This violation constitutes a miracle. Subordinate cause has ceased to function, and supreme cause operates directly upon the world." — Chapter I, 'Unification of Science and Religion', an excerpt from *Evolution of Religion and Science*, by the same author. — (tr.)

# III. ESP ABILITY, CHAKRAS AND MERIDIANS

## —ESP Tests Performed by Dr. Brenio Onetto Bachler[1]—

### A. Objectives

To explore the relationship between ESP (Extra Sensory Perception) ability, Chakras and meridians.

### B. Experimental Procedure

*Number of Subjects*

The number of subjects in this study was thirty.

*Measurements*

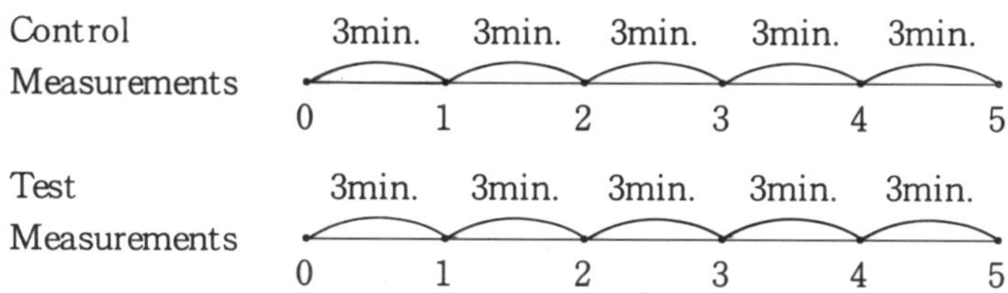


**Diagram Ⅲ- 1**: Experimental Procedure

First, as a control, five measurements of each of the fourteen meridians' function[2] were taken by the AMI[3] at three-minute intervals while the subject was at rest.

Next, five AMI measurements were again taken at three-minute intervals while five ESP test runs[4] were done. A signal was given to the subject by the experimenter to ensure that each of the five ESP test runs would be completed by the end of each three-minute interval (Diagram Ⅲ-1).

*ESP Test Method*

The experimenter placed 25 well-shuffled ESP cards stacked (face down) on a table approximately one meter from the subject. The experimenter then requested the subject to guess the identity of the cards from the bottom of the stack up, and to write each response in the appropriate column on the test sheet. After the subject had attempted to identify the 25 cards, the cards were left stacked in the same order at the edge of the table. This procedure constituted one test run. Another set of well-shuffled cards was then placed on the table and the next ESP test was performed by repeating the same procedure.

After five runs had been completed in this manner, the actual sequence of the cards was written in the designated space next to the responses for each run. The correct answers were tabulated, and the total score for the five runs was calculated.

## C. Division into Classes

Following the parapsychological principles laid down by American parapsychologist J.B. Rhine, the deviation (Dev.), standard deviation (S.D.) and $t = \left|\frac{\text{Dev.}}{\text{S.D.}}\right|$ are calculated from the ESP total score. With this t is determined $\int_0^t \phi(t)dt$ of normal distribution chart. The probability of obtaining a given total score by chance is derived using the equation $P = 1 - \int_0^t \phi(t)\,dt \times 2$. For the subject whose probability of obtaining the score by chance is 1 % or less, the presence of ESP can be inferred.

If this method were followed, none of the thirty subjects could be said to be manifesting ESP ability, nor could any of the subjects be said to be suppressing ESP ability. The highest scorer, K.A. (who has been practicing yogic meditation six or seven hours daily for two years), achieved a score of (only) 33 points. Calculating the probability according to Rhine's methods:

TS (total score) = 33

Dev. = 33 − 25 = 8 (25 is the score obtainable by chance)

S.D. = $\sqrt{125 \times \frac{1}{5} \times \frac{4}{5}}$ = 4.47

t = $\frac{8}{4.47}$ = 1.79

$\int_0^t \phi(t)dt$ = 0.463 (from the normal distribution chart)

P (probability) = 1 − 0.463 × 2 = 0.074

Thus, even by chance, a score of 33 points can be obtained 7.4 times out of 100 trials.

Using Rhine's method, even K.A., the highest scorer of the 30 subjects, could not be said to be exhibiting ESP ability.

As has been previously stated, however, since ancient times ESP ability has been known to be a specific type of Psi ability associated with the Manipura and Svadhishthana Chakras. Even if statistically it cannot be said that ESP ability is at work, if this ability has been exhibited or suppressed even slightly, one can presuppose the possible occurrence of substantial changes in the Ki and function of the meridians associated with the Manipura and Svadhishthana Chakras.

For this reason the 30 subjects were divided into three classes : Those with a deviation of six (score of 31 or more) were placed into the Psi-hit class (exhibiting ESP ability); those with a deviation of minus five (score of 20 or less) were placed into the Psi-miss class (ESP ability suppressed); and those subjects with a deviation of from plus one to minus one (score of 26-24) were placed into the chance-scorer class (ESP ability not exhibited)[5]. The meridians which showed significant changes and their related Chakras were examined in these classes.

## D. Method of Data Processing

**Table Ⅲ − 1**: Psi-hit Class (Dev.≧6) ; 5 subjects

〔 ( L+R )/2 , | L−R | 〕 BP

| | LU | LI | HC | TH | HT | SI | SP | LV | ST | GB | KI | UB | Sum |
|---|---|---|---|---|---|---|---|---|---|---|---|---|---|
| N | 10 | 10 | 9 | 10 | 10 | 9 | 9 | 9 | 10 | 10 | 9 | 10 | 115 |
| C | 0 | 0 | 1 | 0 | 0 | 1 | 1 | 1 | 0 | 0 | 1 | 0 | 5 |
| % | 0.0 | 0.0 | 11.1 | 0.0 | 0.0 | 11.1 | 11.1 | 11.1 | 0.0 | 0.0 | 11.1 | 0.0 | 4.3 |

Notes for tables: N = Frequency of no significant change
C = Frequency of significant change

**Table III − 2**: Psi-miss Class (Dev. ≦-5); 4 subjects

〔 ( L+R )/2 , | L−R | 〕 BP

| | LU | LI | HC | TH | HT | SI | SP | LV | ST | GB | KI | UB | Sum |
|---|---|---|---|---|---|---|---|---|---|---|---|---|---|
| N | 8 | 8 | 7 | 8 | 6 | 8 | 8 | 7 | 7 | 8 | 8 | 7 | 90 |
| C | 0 | 0 | 1 | 0 | 2 | 0 | 0 | 1 | 1 | 0 | 0 | 1 | 6 |
| % | 0.0 | 0.0 | 14.3 | 0.0 | 33.3 | 0.0 | 0.0 | 14.3 | 14.3 | 0.0 | 0.0 | 14.3 | 6.7 |

**Table III − 3**: Chance-scorer Class (-1≦ Dev. ≦+1) ; 6 subjects

〔 ( L+R )/2 , | L−R | 〕 BP

| | LU | LI | HC | TH | HT | SI | SP | LV | ST | GB | KI | UB | Sum |
|---|---|---|---|---|---|---|---|---|---|---|---|---|---|
| N | 10 | 10 | 11 | 12 | 12 | 12 | 12 | 12 | 12 | 12 | 12 | 12 | 139 |
| C | 2 | 2 | 1 | 0 | 0 | 0 | 0 | 0 | 0 | 0 | 0 | 0 | 5 |
| % | 20.0 | 20.0 | 9.1 | 0.0 | 0.0 | 0.0 | 0.0 | 0.0 | 0.0 | 0.0 | 0.0 | 0.0 | 3.6 |

For each class, the averages (AV) of (L+R)/2 and L−R=D of BP values (parameter of meridian function) of five sets of control data and those of (L+R)/2 and L−R=D of BP values of five sets of ESP test data for each meridian were calculated[6]. Then t-tests of the corresponding values were performed to examine whether or not there were significant differences between them, and these results were tabled in Ⅲ-1, 2, and 3.

## E. Analyses and Considerations

### *1. Meridians Indicating Significant Changes*

According to Tables Ⅲ-1, 2 and 3, the meridians exhibiting significant change were, for each class:

Psi-hit class : Heart constrictor, small intestine, spleen, liver, and kidney meridians (Ⅲ-1) ;

Psi-miss class : Heart constrictor, heart, liver, stomach and urinary bladder meridians, (Ⅲ-2) ;

Chance-scorer class : Lung, large intestine, and heart constrictor meridians (Ⅲ-3).

The above suggests :

*a.* The heart constrictor meridian exhibited significant change in all three classes. This change might indicate mental tension due to participation in the ESP tests[7].

*b.* In the Psi-miss class, significant changes occurred in both the heart constrictor and heart meridians, which are related to the Anahata Chakra and the cardiovascular system. These changes indicate that tension was greater in the cardiovascular system in this class than in the other two classes. This tension can be considered a possible negative influence, and could result in the failure of ESP ability, if present, to manifest itself.

*c.* In the chance-scorer class, unlike the other two classes, the meridians associated with the Vishuddhi Chakra, i.e. the lung and large intestine showed significant changes.

*d.* In both the Psi-miss and Psi-hit classes, the kidney, urinary bladder and small intestine meridians (associated with the Svadhishthana Chakra) exhibited significant changes. Moreover, significant changes were observed in the spleen, stomach, and liver meridians (related to the Manipura Chakra).

As explained in Chapter I, the Manipura Chakra has a close connection with ESP ability. The Svadhishthana Chakra has a close relationship with the unconscious and spontaneous ESP ability. It can therefore be surmised that in both the Psi-hit and Psi-miss classes ESP ability, associated with the Manipura and Svadhishthana Chakras, was at work. This data is important support for the empirical basis of the relationship between Chakras and ESP ability.

The Psi-miss and Psi-hit classes differ in that in the Psi-miss class, both the heart and heart constrictor meridians (associated with the Anahata Chakra) showed significant changes, indicating that both these meridians were at work and that there was mental tension. It is conceivable that in the Psi-miss class the greater activity of the Anahata Chakra, whose main function is emission of Psi energy, has an antagonistic influence on ESP ability (the ability to receive Psi energy) and thus suppresses its expression.

*e.* In the chance-scorer class, no significant change was seen in the meridians associated with either the ESP-related Manipura or Svadhishthana Chakras. Thus, neither Chakra is considered to have been active.

### 2. *Nature of the Significant Changes Found in Three Classes*

The meridians which showed significant changes during the ESP test are examined in each class as follows:

*a. Psi-hit class*

For the left/right average, $(L+R)/2$ of the BP values, the Anahata-related heart constrictor meridian showed a significant decrease reflecting both the diminished activity of Ki and function of this meridian. Of the Svadhishthana-related small intestine and kidney meridians, the small intestine meridian showed a significant activity decrease, while the kidney meridian showed a significant increase in activity (Table Ⅲ-4).

**Table Ⅲ - 4**

〔(L+R)/2〕 BP

| | LU | LI | HC | TH | HT | SI | SP | LV | ST | GB | KI | UB | Sum |
|---|---|---|---|---|---|---|---|---|---|---|---|---|---|
| SD | — | — | SD | — | — | SD | — | — | — | — | SD | — | — |
| X | 0.0 | 0.0 | 25.0 | 0.0 | 0.0 | 25.0 | 0.0 | 0.0 | 0.0 | 0.0 | 25.0 | 0.0 | — |
| % | 0.000 | 0.000 | 0.001 | 0.000 | 0.000 | 0.001 | 0.000 | 0.000 | 0.000 | 0.000 | 0.001 | 0.000 | — |
| x | 0.0 | 0.0 | 10.8 | 0.0 | 0.0 | 10.8 | 0.0 | 0.0 | 0.0 | 0.0 | 10.8 | 0.0 | — |

〔(L+R)/2〕 BP

| | LU | LI | (HC) | TH | HT | (SI) | SP | LV | ST | GB | (KI) | UB | Sum |
|---|---|---|---|---|---|---|---|---|---|---|---|---|---|
| D | | | D | | | D | | | | | | | — |
| I | | | | | | | | | | | I | | — |

Notes for tables: SD = Significant difference
X = $\chi 2$ test value
% = Closest significance level to the above $\chi 2$ test value
x = Value of the above significance level
D = Decrease
I = Increase

For the left/right imbalance, L−R=D of the BP values, the Manipura-related spleen meridian exhibited a significant increase, which indicates imbalance between the right and left branches. Contrary to this imbalance, the Manipura-related liver meridian showed a significant decrease, indicating an improved balance (Table Ⅲ-5).

**Table Ⅲ - 5**

〔| L−R |〕 BP

| | LU | LI | HC | TH | HT | SI | SP | LV | ST | GB | KI | UB | Sum |
|---|---|---|---|---|---|---|---|---|---|---|---|---|---|
| | — | — | — | — | — | — | SD | SD | — | — | — | — | — |
| X | 0.0 | 0.0 | 0.0 | 0.0 | 0.0 | 0.0 | 25.0 | 25.0 | 0.0 | 0.0 | 0.0 | 0.0 | — |
| % | 0.000 | 0.000 | 0.000 | 0.000 | 0.000 | 0.000 | 0.001 | 0.001 | 0.000 | 0.000 | 0.000 | 0.000 | — |
| x | 0.0 | 0.0 | 0.0 | 0.0 | 0.0 | 0.0 | 10.8 | 10.8 | 0.0 | 0.0 | 0.0 | 0.0 | — |

〔| L−R |〕 BP

| | LU | LI | HC | TH | HT | SI | (SP) | (LV) | ST | GB | KI | UB | Sum |
|---|---|---|---|---|---|---|---|---|---|---|---|---|---|
| D | | | | | | | | D | | | | | — |
| I | | | | | | | I | | | | | | — |

*b. Psi-miss class*

For the (L+R)/2 of the BP values a significant decrease in both the Anahata-related heart constrictor and heart meridians, reflecting a decrease in meridian function and Ki, was seen. There was a significant increase in the Manipura-related liver meridian, as well as a significant decrease in the Manipura-related stomach and the Svadhishthana-related urinary bladder meridians (Table Ⅲ-6).

No significant change was noted for the L−R=D of the BP values (Table Ⅲ-7).

**Table Ⅲ − 6**

〔(L+R)/2〕 BP

| | LU | LI | HC | TH | HT | SI | SP | LV | ST | GB | KI | UB | Sum |
|---|---|---|---|---|---|---|---|---|---|---|---|---|---|
| SD | — | — | SD | — | SD | — | — | SD | SD | — | — | SD | — |
| X | 0.0 | 0.0 | 33.3 | 0.0 | 100.0 | 0.0 | 0.0 | 33.3 | 33.3 | 0.0 | 0.0 | 33.3 | — |
| % | 0.000 | 0.000 | 0.001 | 0.000 | 0.001 | 0.000 | 0.000 | 0.001 | 0.001 | 0.000 | 0.000 | 0.001 | — |
| x | 0.0 | 0.0 | 10.8 | 0.0 | 10.8 | 0.0 | 0.0 | 10.8 | 10.8 | 0.0 | 0.0 | 10.8 | — |

〔(L+R)/2〕 BP

| | LU | LI | (HC) | TH | (HT) | SI | SP | (LV) | (ST) | GB | KI | (UB) | Sum |
|---|---|---|---|---|---|---|---|---|---|---|---|---|---|
| D | | | D | | D | | | | D | | | D | — |
| I | | | | | | | | I | | | | | — |

**Table Ⅲ − 7**

〔|L−R|〕 BP

| | LU | LI | HC | TH | HT | SI | SP | LV | ST | GB | KI | UB | Sum |
|---|---|---|---|---|---|---|---|---|---|---|---|---|---|
| SD | — | — | — | — | — | — | — | — | — | — | — | — | — |
| X | 0.0 | 0.0 | 0.0 | 0.0 | 0.0 | 0.0 | 0.0 | 0.0 | 0.0 | 0.0 | 0.0 | 0.0 | — |
| % | 0.000 | 0.000 | 0.000 | 0.000 | 0.000 | 0.000 | 0.000 | 0.000 | 0.000 | 0.000 | 0.000 | 0.000 | — |
| x | 0.0 | 0.0 | 0.0 | 0.0 | 0.0 | 0.0 | 0.0 | 0.0 | 0.0 | 0.0 | 0.0 | 0.0 | — |

〔|L−R|〕 BP

| | LU | LI | HC | TH | HT | SI | SP | LV | ST | GB | KI | UB | Sum |
|---|---|---|---|---|---|---|---|---|---|---|---|---|---|
| D | | | | | | | | | | | | | — |
| I | | | | | | | | | | | | | — |

*c. Chance-scorer Class*

For the (L+R)/2 of the BP values, a significant decrease was indicated in the Vishuddhi-related lung and large intestine meridians. For the L − R = D of the BP values, a significant increase of imbalance was seen in the Vishuddhi-related large intestine meridian and also in the Anahata-related heart constrictor meridian (Tables Ⅲ-8 & 9).

**Table Ⅲ − 8**

〔(L+R)/2〕 BP

| | LU | LI | HC | TH | HT | SI | SP | LV | ST | GB | KI | UB | Sum |
|---|---|---|---|---|---|---|---|---|---|---|---|---|---|
| SD | SD | SD | — | — | — | — | — | — | — | — | — | — | — |
| X | 50.0 | 20.0 | 0.0 | 0.0 | 0.0 | 0.0 | 0.0 | 0.0 | 0.0 | 0.0 | 0.0 | 0.0 | — |
| % | 0.001 | 0.001 | 0.000 | 0.000 | 0.000 | 0.000 | 0.000 | 0.000 | 0.000 | 0.000 | 0.000 | 0.000 | — |
| x | 10.8 | 10.8 | 0.0 | 0.0 | 0.0 | 0.0 | 0.0 | 0.0 | 0.0 | 0.0 | 0.0 | 0.0 | — |

〔(L+R)/2〕 BP

| | (LU) | (LI) | HC | TH | HT | SI | SP | LV | ST | GB | KI | UB | Sum |
|---|---|---|---|---|---|---|---|---|---|---|---|---|---|
| D | D | D | | | | | | | | | | | — |
| I | | | | | | | | | | | | | — |

**Table Ⅲ − 9**

〔| L−R |〕 BP

| | LU | LI | HC | TH | HT | SI | SP | LV | ST | GB | KI | UB | Sum |
|---|---|---|---|---|---|---|---|---|---|---|---|---|---|
| SD | — | SD | SD | — | — | — | — | — | — | — | — | — | — |
| X | 0.0 | 20.0 | 20.0 | 0.0 | 0.0 | 0.0 | 0.0 | 0.0 | 0.0 | 0.0 | 0.0 | 0.0 | — |
| % | 0.000 | 0.001 | 0.001 | 0.000 | 0.000 | 0.000 | 0.000 | 0.000 | 0.000 | 0.000 | 0.000 | 0.000 | — |
| x | 0.0 | 10.8 | 10.8 | 0.0 | 0.0 | 0.0 | 0.0 | 0.0 | 0.0 | 0.0 | 0.0 | 0.0 | — |

〔| L−R |〕 BP

| | LU | (LI) | (HC) | TH | HT | SI | SP | LV | ST | GB | KI | UB | Sum |
|---|---|---|---|---|---|---|---|---|---|---|---|---|---|
| D | | | | | | | | | | | | | — |
| I | | I | I | | | | | | | | | | — |

### *3. Comparison of Significant Changes between the Three Classes*

*a. Meridians Related to the Anahata Chakra*

Although the heart constrictor meridian exhibited significant change in all three classes, upon comparison of the classes the following differences were noted. In both the Psi-hit and Psi-miss classes, a significant decrease in meridian function and Ki was observed. In contrast, the right/left imbalance of this meridian significantly increased in the chance-scorer class.

A significant decrease of function and Ki was also seen in the heart meridian in the Psi-miss class.

*b. Meridians Related to the Manipura Chakra*

A significant increase in the left/right imbalance in the spleen meridian, and a significant decrease in the left/right imbalance in the liver meridian were seen in the Psi-hit class. In the Psi-miss class, a significant increase in meridian function and Ki was seen in the liver meridian, and a significant decrease noted in the stomach meridian's function and Ki.

*c. Meridians Related to the Svadhishthana Chakra*

A significant increase in function and Ki in the kidney meridian, and a significant decrease in function and Ki in the small intestine meridian were observed in the Psi-hit class.

In the Psi-miss class, a significant decrease of function and Ki was seen in the urinary bladder meridian.

*d. Merdians Related to the Vishuddhi Chakra*

Significant changes in these meridians were only observed in the chance-scorer class : A decrease of function and Ki in the lung and large intestine meridians, and an increase of the left/right imbalance in the large intestine meridian.

## F. Conclusion of Chapter III

*1.* In contrast to the chance-scorer class, both the Psi-hit and Psi-miss classes showed significant changes in the meridians associated with the Manipura and Svadhishthana Chakras, which are empirically known to be closely connected with ESP ability : There were significant changes in the Manipura-related spleen, stomach, and liver meridians as well as in the Svadhishthana-related kidney, urinary bladder, and small intestine meridians.

In the chance-scorer class, which did not exhibit the presence of ESP ability, significant change was not observed in the meridians related to the Manipura and Svadhishthana Chakras. Significant change was only noted in the lung and large intestine meridians, related to the Vishuddhi Chakra, which is not closely associated with ESP ability.

*2.* A significant change in the Anahata-related heart constrictor meridian is common to all three classes. Both the heart constrictor and heart meridians, as well as the heart itself, readily undergo functional changes when people are anxious and ill at ease. Therefore, the people in all three classes are thought to have experienced mental tension as a result of undertaking ESP testing.

*3.* In the Psi-miss class, significant changes were seen in the heart meridian as well as the heart constrictor. The subjects in this class seem to have experienced the most tension. This tension is a possible explanation for the failure of ESP ability, even though present, to manifest itself and the resulting ESP suppression.

*4.* Comparing the nature of the significant changes seen in the meridians in the three classes does not reveal distinct differences. Nonetheless, the notable characteristics and variations among the three classes, however slight, were examined:

*a.* Of the meridians related to the Anahata Chakra, the heart constrictor meridian exhibited significant change in all three classes : A decrease of function and Ki in this meridian in the Psi-hit and Psi-miss classes ; and in contrast, an increase of imbalance in the chance-scorer class.

The awakening and activation of the Chakras is thought to be accompanied by increased function and Ki in the related meridians. Thus the decrease in the function and Ki of the heart constrictor meridian in both the Psi-hit and Psi-miss classes might be interpreted as a decrease in activity of the Anahata Chakra when ESP ability is at work, and unstable function (indicated by increased right/left imblance of the related meridian function) in the Anahata Chakra when ESP ability is not exhibited. However, as is seen in the case of the Psi-miss class, when the functional decrease in the Anahata Chakra (reflected in the heart and heart constrictor meridian fucntion) is too extreme, ESP ability might conversely seem to be suppressed rather than activated.

*b*. Of the meridians associated with the Manipura Chakra the ones considered most closely related, from empirical and clinical observation, are the spleen and stomach meridians. Comparing these two meridians as observed in the Psi-hit and Psi-miss classes, a significant increase in the left/right imbalance was seen in the spleen meridian in the Psi-hit class; on the other hand, a significant decrease of Ki and meridian function was seen in the stomach meridian in the Psi-miss class. Although the change seen in the (L+R)/2 of the spleen meridian was not significant in the Psi-hit class, still, certain tendencies could be observed : Three of the five Psi-hit class members showed an increase of function and Ki (t values of the five were : −0.281, +0.179, −0.272, +0.074, +0.221). This increase might seem to indicate that when the spleen meridian exhibits an increase and an imbalance, ESP ability is more easily activated ; in a like manner, when the stomach meridian shows a decrease, ESP activity is likely to be suppressed.

*c*. Of the meridians associated with the Svadhishthana Chakra, the kidney and urinary bladder meridians are considered the ones most closely related in both empirical and clinical observation. Comparing these meridians as seen in the Psi-hit and Psi-miss classes, a significant increase in Ki and meridian function is seen in the kidney meridian in the Psi-hit class; whereas a significant decrease in Ki and meridian function is observed in the urinary bladder meridian in the Psi-miss class. This observation leads to the speculation that when ESP ability is activated the kidney meridian function and Ki energy increases, and when the Ki energy and function of the urinary bladder meridian decreases, ESP ability is suppressed.

From the results of this ESP test only, it is not clear whether activated ESP ability is in the domain of the Manipura Chakra, the Svadhishthana Chakra, or both Chakras. At present it may only be surmised as the result of the joint activity of both Chakras.

In the next chapter, an experiment conducted to verify the actual existence of PK (psychokinetic) phenomena will be discussed.

Notes for Chapter Ⅲ

1) *Brenio Onetto Bachler, M.D., Ph.D.*: Dr Onetto was formerly a Professor of Parapsychology at the University of Chile's Psychology Department. He came to the Institute for Religious Psychology as a recipient of the Motoyama-Bentov Research Fellowship, established by Dr Motoyama to assist promising scientists who wished to study human existence in its holistic sense. He stayed from November 1983 to January 1984. He and the Institute staff conducted research on ESP ability with the AMI. (tr.)

2) See note (1)-(*e*) of Chapter Ⅱ. (tr.)

3) See note (1) of Chapter Ⅱ (tr.)

4) *ESP Tests*: The ESP test used in this study was that developed by the American parapsychologist, J.B. Rhine: A set of 25 cards with square, circle, cross, wavy lines, and asterisk sysmbols. (tr.)

5) The test results of the fifteen subjects whose scores were in-between these criteria were ignored for this evaluation. (tr.)

6) $(L+R)/2$ : The value obtained by dividing the sum of the left and right BP values by two for each meridian. It is a parameter reflecting the average of the function and level of Ki in the left and right branches of each meridian.
$L-R=D$: The absolute difference (D %) between the left and right BP (L %, R %) values of each meridian. It is a parameter indicating the balance of function and Ki level between the left and right branches. The higher the D value, the greater is the imbalance between left and right functioning in each meridian.

7) It has been known that the heart and heart constrictor meridians, along with the function of the heart itself, readily undergo functional change when people are in a mentally anxious and unrestful condition. These are the meridians that are commonly used for the treatment of mental and emotional disturbances in acupuncture clinics. (tr.)

# IV. PK(PSYCHOKINESIS) TESTS AND MERIDIAN FUNCTION

## A. Objectives

The objectives were to explore which meridians correlate with PK (Psychokinetic) abilities, which are associated with the Ajna Chakra[1]; and to evidence the existence of PK ability and PK energy by examining significant functional changes occurring in the meridians that are closely connected to the acupuncture points of the recipient to which PK energy was directed.

## B. Experimental Procedure

First, the meridian function and Ki condition of the fourteen meridians of the recipient[2] were monitored with the AMI. After this measurement, the recipient left the experiment room (Diagram Ⅳ-1).

The sender[3] then entered the room, and his meridian function was monitored. Keeping the electrodes in place, his meridian function was monitored consecutively ten times at 30-second intervals. Within one minute after the end of the tenth measurement, the recipient re-entered the room

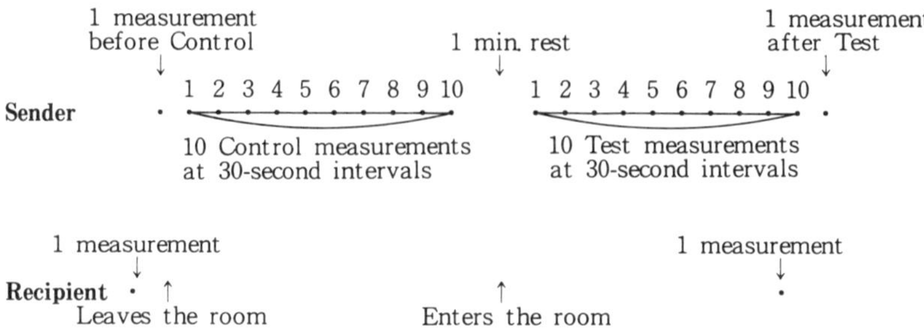


**Diagram Ⅳ - 1**: Experimental Procedure

and sat on a chair placed two meters from the sender. (The sender took a one-minute rest for energy emission.) After the rest, with the electrodes still in place, the sender emitted Psi energy from the Ajna Chakra to the lower abdomen of the recipient, directing his energy for five minutes to Chukyoku (Chungchi in Chinese), CV3, the alarm point of the urinary bladder meridian, and Kangen (Kuanyuan in Chinese), CV4, the alarm point of the small intestine meridian. During this energy emission, the sender's meridian functions were monitored ten times at 30 second intervals. After these measurements were completed, the sender's meridian functions were again monitored. Finally, the meridian function of the recipient was monitored.

This process constituted one run of the PK test. Five runs were repeated under the same conditions between 1:00 - 2 : 30 pm, (before lunch) every day for five days.

## C. Data Assessment

### *1. Data of the Sender*

For each run, the averages of the ten sets of control data for $(L+R)/2$ and $L-R=D$ of the BP values of each meridian were calculated. The same averages for the ten sets of test data (during Psi energy emission) were calculated. T-tests were then performed between the corresponding values for each (L+R)/2 and L−R=D to examine whether or not there was any significant difference between the average values of the ten sets of control data and the ten sets of test data.

With this method, the sum total of the frequency of significant change (C) and insignificant change (N) for (L+R)/2 and L−R=D of each meridian was calculated for five consecutive test runs. The results are listed in Table Ⅳ-1[4].

**Table Ⅳ − 1**: Sum Frequencies of Significant Change for (L+R)/2 and L−R=D and Those of No Change (Insignificant)

| | LU | LI | (HC) | TH | HT | SI | (SP) | LV | (ST) | GB | KI | (UB) |
|---|---|---|---|---|---|---|---|---|---|---|---|---|
| N | 8 | 7 | 5 | 8 | 9 | 7 | 5 | 6 | 5 | 9 | 7 | 1 |
| C | 2 | 3 | (5) | 2 | 1 | 3 | (5) | 4 | (5) | 1 | 3 | (9) |

($\chi^2 = 23.88 > \chi^2 (r = .05) = 19.68$ df=11)

Notes for tables : N =Frequency of no significant change
C =Frequency of significant change

On the basis of this table, $\chi^2$ tests were performed to examine how the frequency distribution of 'change' and 'no change' differed among the twelve meridians.

From the t-tests and the $\chi^2$ tests, which of the sender's meridians underwent significant changes by the emission of PK energy from the Ajna Chakra was to be examined. Furthermore, through this test analyses and the recipient's test analyses, whether or not PK energy was actually emitted and generated significant changes in the recipient's meridian function could be determined.

### *2. Data of the Recipient*

The average of the measurements for five runs for (L+R)/2 of the BP values for each meridian taken before the sender directed PK energy to the lower abdomen 〔(CV3) and (CV4) of the recipient〕 was calculated. The same average after PK energy emission was also calculated. To examine whether or not any significant change occurred in the recipient's meridian function, t-tests were performed between the corresponding values and a table was compiled in order to classify the meridians that underwent significant changes and those which did not. T-tests were also performed to examine whether or not there was any significant difference between the average of the BP values for all fourteen meridians (parameter of the entire level of Ki) in the five measurements before and after PK energy emission. The latter t-tests were to examine the change in the entire meridian function of the recipient after PK energy emission.

## D. Analyses and Discussion

### *1. Data of the Sender*

#### *a. Meridians that Displayed Significant Changes*

In Table Ⅳ-1, the frequency distribution for the meridians that displayed significant change (and those that did not) reveals a significant difference at the level of 5 %. This indicates that some of the meridians underwent significant changes with high frequency while others did not.

The frequency of significant change was most conspicuous in the urinary bladder meridian. This meridian begins its flow in the proximity of the physical location of the Ajna Chakra. In our empirical and clinical experience it is this meridian, together with the governor vessel meridian, which is closely connected to the Ajna Chakra.

This meridian shows the most frequent significant change, evidencing the close connection between the Ajna Chakra and the urinary bladder meridian. The small intestine meridian, which passes Ki into the urinary bladder meridian in the proximity of the location of the Ajna Chakra, showed significant changes with a ratio of three to ten, although this change is less than a nine out of ten ratio for the urinary bladder meridian.

Following the urinary bladder meridian, significant change with high frequency was recorded in the heart constrictor meridian (which is related to the Anahata Chakra) and the spleen and stomach meridians (which are in turn related to the Manipura Chakra).

The Anahata Chakra is empirically known as the Chakra which emits energy outside the body. PK energy may also have been emitted from the Anahata Chakra when it was emitted from the Ajna Chakra. The frequent recording of the significant change in the Manipura-related stomach and spleen meridians may be due to the constitution of the sender of this experiment (H.M.), who easily develops functional changes in these Manipura-related meridians, and whose Manipura Chakra is very active.

### *b. Nature of Significant Change*

**Table Ⅳ − 2**

〔(L+R)/2〕 BP

| | LU | LI | HC | TH | HT | SI | SP | LV | ST | GB | KI | UB | Sum |
|---|---|---|---|---|---|---|---|---|---|---|---|---|---|
| N | 4 | 4 | 2 | 4 | 5 | 3 | 2 | 3 | 4 | 4 | 3 | 0 | 38 |
| C | 1 | 1 | 3 | 1 | 0 | 2 | 3 | 2 | 1 | 1 | 2 | 5 | 22 |
| D | 0 | 0 | 0 | 1 | 0 | 2 | 3 | 2 | 1 | 1 | 2 | 2 | 14 |
| I | 1 | 1 | 3 | 0 | 0 | 0 | 0 | 0 | 0 | 0 | 0 | 3 | 8 |

〔(L+R)/2〕 BP

| | LU | LI | HC | TH | HT | SI | SP | LV | ST | GB | KI | UB | Sum |
|---|---|---|---|---|---|---|---|---|---|---|---|---|---|
| C | 25.0 | 25.0 | 150.0 | 25.0 | 0.0 | 66.7 | 150.0 | 66.7 | 25.0 | 25.0 | 66.7 | 999.9 | 57.9 |
| D | 0.0 | 0.0 | 0.0 | 25.0 | 0.0 | 66.7 | 150.0 | 66.7 | 25.0 | 25.0 | 66.7 | 999.9 | 36.8 |
| I | 25.0 | 25.0 | 150.0 | 0.0 | 0.0 | 0.0 | 0.0 | 0.0 | 0.0 | 0.0 | 0.0 | 999.9 | 21.1 |

〔(L+R)/2〕 BP

| | LU | LI | HC | TH | HT | SI | SP | LV | ST | GB | KI | UB | Sum |
|---|---|---|---|---|---|---|---|---|---|---|---|---|---|
| SD | — | — | SD | — | — | SD | SD | SD | — | — | SD | SD | — |
| X | 0.0 | 0.0 | 150.0 | 0.0 | 0.0 | 66.7 | 150.0 | 66.7 | 0.0 | 0.0 | 66.7 | 200.0 | — |
| % | 0.000 | 0.000 | 0.001 | 0.000 | 0.000 | 0.001 | 0.001 | 0.001 | 0.000 | 0.000 | 0.001 | 0.001 | — |
| x | 0.0 | 0.0 | 0.0 | 0.0 | 0.0 | 10.8 | 10.8 | 10.8 | 0.0 | 0.0 | 10.8 | 10.8 | — |

〔(L+R)/2〕 BP

| | LU | LI | (HC) | TH | HT | (SI) | (SP) | (LV) | ST | GB | (KI) | (UB) | Sum |
|---|---|---|---|---|---|---|---|---|---|---|---|---|---|
| D | | | | | | D | D | D | | | D | | — |
| I | | | I | | | | | | | | | I | — |

Table Ⅳ-2 examines the nature of significant change, both toward the increase of the BP value (activation of meridian function and increase of Ki) and toward the decrease of the BP value (deterioration of meridian function and decrease of Ki). As for (L+R)/2, the frequency of significant change (C) was sub-classified into Decrease (D) and Increase (I). An $x^2$ test was performed for each of the twelve meridians in order to establish whether or not there was any significant difference between the frequency of the increase and that of the decrease.

Similarly, the frequency of increase and decrease was

**Table Ⅳ - 3**

〔| L-R |〕 BP

| | LU | LI | HC | TH | HT | SI | SP | LV | ST | GB | KI | UB | Sum |
|---|---|---|---|---|---|---|---|---|---|---|---|---|---|
| N | 4 | 3 | 3 | 4 | 4 | 4 | 3 | 3 | 1 | 5 | 4 | 1 | 39 |
| C | 1 | 2 | 2 | 1 | 1 | 1 | 2 | 2 | 4 | 0 | 1 | 4 | 21 |
| D | 1 | 1 | 0 | 0 | 0 | 1 | 1 | 1 | 1 | 0 | 1 | 2 | 9 |
| I | 0 | 1 | 2 | 1 | 1 | 0 | 1 | 1 | 3 | 0 | 0 | 2 | 12 |

〔| L-R |〕 BP

| | LU | LI | HC | TH | HT | SI | SP | LV | ST | GB | KI | UB | Sum |
|---|---|---|---|---|---|---|---|---|---|---|---|---|---|
| C | 25.0 | 66.7 | 66.7 | 25.0 | 25.0 | 25.0 | 66.7 | 66.7 | 400.0 | 0.0 | 25.0 | 400.0 | 53.8 |
| D | 25.0 | 33.3 | 0.0 | 0.0 | 0.0 | 25.0 | 33.3 | 33.3 | 100.0 | 0.0 | 25.0 | 200.0 | 23.1 |
| I | 0.0 | 33.3 | 66.7 | 25.0 | 25.0 | 0.0 | 33.3 | 33.3 | 300.0 | 0.0 | 0.0 | 200.0 | 30.8 |

〔| L-R |〕 BP

| | LU | LI | HC | TH | HT | SI | SP | LV | ST | GB | KI | UB | Sum |
|---|---|---|---|---|---|---|---|---|---|---|---|---|---|
| SD | — | — | SD | — | — | — | — | — | SD | — | — | — | — |
| X | 0.0 | 0.0 | 66.7 | 0.0 | 0.0 | 0.0 | 0.0 | 0.0 | 100.0 | 0.0 | 0.0 | 0.0 | — |
| % | 0.000 | 0.000 | 0.001 | 0.000 | 0.000 | 0.000 | 0.000 | 0.000 | 0.001 | 0.000 | 0.000 | 0.000 | — |
| x | 0.0 | 0.0 | 10.8 | 0.0 | 0.0 | 0.0 | 0.0 | 0.0 | 10.8 | 0.0 | 0.0 | 0.0 | — |

〔| L-R |〕 BP

| | LU | LI | (HC) | TH | HT | SI | SP | LV | (ST) | GB | KI | UB | Sum |
|---|---|---|---|---|---|---|---|---|---|---|---|---|---|
| D | | | | | | | | | | | | | — |
| I | | | I | | | | | | I | | | | — |

Notes for tables : N = Frequency of no significant change
C = Frequency of significant change
D = Decrease
I = Increase
SD = Significant difference
X = $\chi 2$ test value
% = Closest significance level to the above $\chi 2$ test value
x = Value of the above significance level

classified for L − R = D (difference between left and right). An $x^2$ test was also performed for each of the twelve meridians (Table Ⅳ-3).

The $x^2$ test did not yield any significant difference between I and D for (L + R)/2 and L − R = D. Since this may be due to a small number of samplings, the frequencies of I and D were respectively divided by the frequency of no significant change (N) for each meridian and the rate of change (% value) was calculated by multiplying the obtained value by one hundred in order to examine the direction of I and D. $x^2$ tests were then done for this rate of change (Tables Ⅳ-2 and Ⅳ-3).

In Table Ⅳ-2 for (L + R)/2, the decrease was recorded in the Manipura-related spleen and liver meridians, Svadhishthana-related kidney meridian and Ajna- and Svadhishthana-related small intestine meridian; and the increase was in the Anahata-related heart constrictor meridian and Ajna- and Svadhishthana-related urinary bladder meridian.

Table Ⅳ-3 for L − R = D indicates that the left-right imbalance increased in the Anahata-related heart-constrictor meridian and the Manipura-related stomach meridian.

*c. Summary*

Decrease of Ki and meridian function was recorded in the spleen and liver meridians, which are closely related to the Manipura Chakra. The main function of this Chakra is the reception of Psi energy. Contrary to this decrease, an increase of Ki and meridian function was recorded in the heart constrictor meridian, which is in a close relation to the Anahata Chakra. The function of this Chakra is mainly the emission of Psi (PK) energy. Furthermore, the most frequent significant change and increase of Ki and Ki functioning, was recorded in the urinary bladder meridian. This meridian begins its flow in the proximity of the Ajna Chakra and seems to indicate that the Psi energy emission from the Ajna Chakra activated the function of this Chakra and the corresponding urinary bladder meridian.

The following section discusses the influence of Psi energy on the recipient's meridian function when the energy is directed from the sender's Ajna Chakra to the recipient's lower abdomen.

## *2. Data of the Recipient*

| | | | | |
|---|---|---|---|---|
| LU | t | = | 1. 4791 | |
| LI | t | = | 2. 6872 | (≒2. 77) |
| HC | t | = | 0. 6654 | |
| DI | t | = | 2. 5904 | |
| TH | t | = | 1. 4125 | |
| HT | t | = | 1. 1188 | |
| SI | t | = | 1. 1829 | |
| SP | t | = | −0. 0245 | |
| LV | t | = | 4. 4071 | (>2. 77) |
| ST | t | = | 0. 6656 | |
| SB | t | = | 0. 7270 | |
| GB | t | = | 0. 7769 | |
| KI | t | = | 0. 8601 | |
| UB | t | = | 1. 5941 | |

df = 4

$t_{.05}$ = 2. 77 $t_{.025}$ = 3. 49

Average t = 1. 6010

**Table Ⅳ - 4**: T-tests Analyses

Referring to Table Ⅳ-4, t = 2.68 of the large intestine meridian does not arrive at 2.77, the 5 % significance level; similarly t = 1.59 of the urinary bladder meridian and t = 1.18 of the small intestine meridian do not arrive at the 5 % significance level.

However, t = 4.40 > $t_{.025}$ = 3.49 of the liver meridian shows significant difference at the 2.5% significance level. That is, after Psi energy emission from the sender's Ajna Chakra a significant increase of the meridian functioning and Ki was recorded in the liver meridian. The sender directed Psi energy into the Chukyoku (CV3 : alarm point of the urinary bladder meridian) and Kangen (CV4 : alarm point of the small intestine meridian) points in the lower abdomen, but no significant change was recorded even at the 5 % significance level in either the urinary bladder or the small intestine meridians. Contrary to these findings, significant change was recorded in the liver meridian. Is there any connection between the liver meridian and the Chukyoku (CV3) and Kangen (CV4) points?

Refer to Figure Ⅳ-1. Acupuncture classics state that the Chukyoku and Kangen points are closely related to the

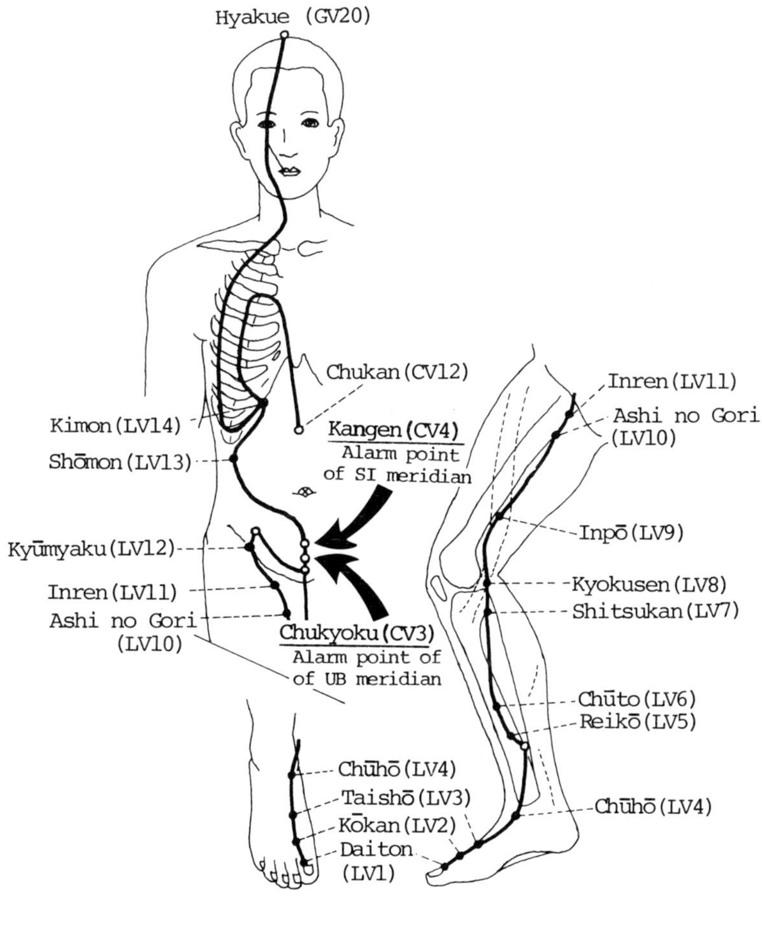


**Figure Ⅳ - 1 :** Liver Meridian

liver meridian : The course of the inner branch of this meridian includes these points and passes the urogenital organs in the lower abdomen. The close functional connection between the liver meridian and the urogenital system is empirically and clinically known in Oriental medicine.

It can therefore be surmised that the Psi energy emitted from the Ajna Chakra of the sender generated (in the recipient) an increased functioning and Ki in the liver meridian, by way of the Kangen and Chukyoku points.

The recipient reported that symptoms of cystitis and urethritis, which she had had for two weeks, disappeared after the first run of this test.

The average of (L+R)/2 of the BP values for all fourteen meridians for five runs before emission, and that of five runs after emission, was calculated in order to examine changes occurring in the overall function of the recipient's meridians as a result of Psi energy emission into the Chukyoku (CV3) and Kangen (CV4) points. The t-tests done between these averages before (control) and after emission (test) shows Average T = 1.60, as indicated in Table Ⅳ-4. This t = 1.60 does not arrive at the 5 % significance level, but indicates an increase of BP values in the fourteen meridians, that is, the increase of functioning and Ki in the entire meridian system of the recipient after energy emission.

## E. Conclusion of Chapter Ⅳ

*1.* When the sender emitted Psi energy from the Ajna Chakra, his urinary bladder meridian, which starts its flow in the vicinity of the Ajna Chakra, showed a significant change with very high frequency. The nature of this significant change was an increase of Ki and functioning of this meridian. It can be surmised as a result of this data that there is a close connection between the PK ability of the Ajna Chakra and the urinary bladder meridian.

2. The sender directed Psi energy from the Ajna Chakra to the area of both the Chukyoku (CV3) and Kangen (CV4) points of the recipient. The liver meridian, the inner branch of which courses through these points and which is closely related to the urogenital system, showed a significant change (increase) with a high significance level. Although the mechanism is as of yet unknown and indirect, this finding is objective and constitutes scientific evidence that suggests:

*a.* Psi energy was actually emitted from the Ajna Chakra of the sender.

*b.* This energy generated the increase of Ki and functioning at a significant level in the meridian related to the acupoints where the energy was directed. In other words, a PK phenomenon occurred.

In this and previous chapters, the relationships among Chakras, Psi energy, meridians and Ki have been discussed based on experiments conducted on Psi, PK, and ESP phenomena.

In the next chapter, an experiment conducted in order to investigate the mutual influence of external Ki, a phenomenon similar to a PK phenomeon, will be discussed.

Notes for Chapter Ⅳ

1) *Ajna Chakra*: The physical location of the Ajna Chakra is said to be between the eyebrows. In acupuncture theory, the course of the governor vessel meridian runs through this area, and in the proximity of its physical location, Ki enters the urinary bladder meridian from the small intestine meridian. (tr.)

2) *Recipient*: The recipient of this experiment was a 51-year-old female. She had a constitution which was conductive to the development of inflammation in the urogenital system, and had suffered from cystitis and urethritis two weeks before the first trial of this experiment. (tr.)

3) *Sender*: The sender in this experiment is the author of this paper (male, age 61 at the time) who has both strong PK and ESP ability and has undergone religious practice for over half a century.

4) Although the functional condition of the fourteen meridians (twelve are regular and two are independent) is monitored with the AMI, the computer analysis for $x^2$ tests are programmed for the twelve regular meridians only, as the running course and nature of the two independent meridians (stomach branch and diaphragm meridians) has not been described in detail in any of the acupuncture texts. Evidence of their existence has not yet been clearly established, thus their exclusion from the analyses. (tr.)

---

# V. THE MUTUAL INFLUENCE OF KI BETWEEN PEOPLE

## A. Objectives

Oriental medicine states that the vital force (called Ki in Chinese medicine and Prana in Yoga) which maintains the life of an organism flows through the body by way of meridians or Nadis. Ki which flows in an organism is called ' internal Ki '. The counterpart of internal Ki[1] is ' external Ki', which is emitted outside the body. The Chinese Chi Gon (or Prana therapy) is one of the techniques in which external Ki is effectively used for treatment. For instance, Chi Gon studies demonstrated that a master using Chi Gon techniques may, without using needles or touching the subject's body, obtain the same results as would acupuncture treatment and needle anesthesia. The Chi Gon master obtained these results by ejecting Ki from his fingers into the subject's meridians through acupoints.

The objective of this experiment is to investigate whether or not such mutual influence of external Ki actually exists. Hereafter, external Ki is simply referred to as Ki.

## B. Experimental Procedure

Sei point[2] active electrodes were first placed on the tips of the subject's limbs (subject 1). After pressing the start button for the AMI measurements, the experimenter left the room.

In a relaxed state, the meridian functions and Ki of subject 1 were monitored ten times at one-minute intervals as a control set. Another subject (subject 2) then entered the room and sat on a chair placed 50-60cm away from subject 1. Both subjects remained quiet in this position for five minutes. After five minutes had passed from the time of subject 2's entrance, the meridian functioning of subject 1 was automatically monitored ten times at one-minute intervals according to the computer program. The electrodes remained on subject 1 throughout the experiment.

To avoid the mutual influence of Ki between subject 1 and the experimenter, the experimenter left the experiment room just after having placed the electrodes on subject 1 and having pressed the start button, and did not re-enter the room until all measurements had been completed. The five-minute period between the control and test measurements ensured a sufficient period for mutual Ki influence between subjects 1 and 2.

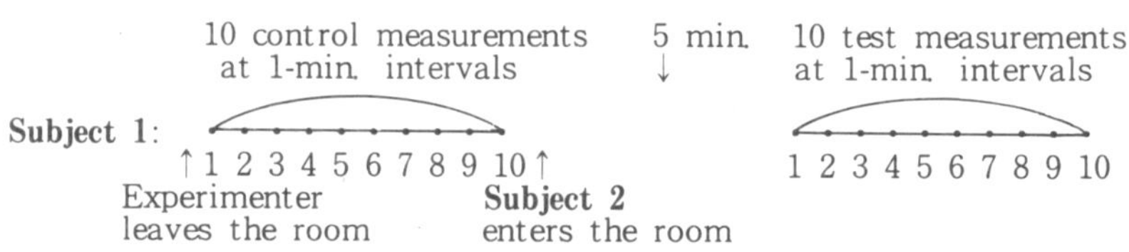


**Diagram V - 1:** Experimental Procedure

This process constituted the first experiment (Diagram V-1). The second experiment was conducted immediately afterward using the same pair of subjects. This time, the meridian function of subject 2 (not previously measured) was monitored ten times as a control set and another ten times as a test following the same procedure described above. This time, subject 1 assumed the role of subject 2 in the first experiment.

## C. Method for Data Analyses

### *1. Covariance Analyses of Six Groups Formed from Ten Individuals in Order of Application Number*

**Table V − 1:**

| | G1 | | G2 | | ・・・・・・・ | G10 | |
|---|---|---|---|---|---|---|---|
| 1 | X11 | Y11 | X21 | Y21 | | X101 | Y101 |
| 2 | X12 | Y12 | X22 | Y22 | | X102 | Y102 |
| ⋮ | | | | | | | |
| 10 | X110 | Y110 | X210 | Y210 | | X1010 | Y1010 |

The subjects were divided into six groups in order of application: the first group being composed of those with the application numbers 1-10 ; the second with the application numbers 11-20 ; and so on through those with the application numbers 51-60. The control data of (L+R)/2 and L−R=D of the BP values[3] of each meridian for each group respectively were assigned in the X column (X1-X10) and the test data of these values in the Y column (Y1-Y10). This information is given in Table V-1.

The covariance analyses were performed with each value in the X and Y columns. The effect on the twelve meridians of the mutual influence of Ki between the subjects was analyzed and discussed.

### 2. *Covariance Analyses of the Normal Meridians*

These covariance analyses were performed for three normal meridians (of the twelve) of each subject for each group in order to examine whether or not the influence of Ki between subjects more easily occurred in normal meridians.

### 3. *Covariance Analyses of the Abnormal Meridians*

The covariance analyses were performed for the four abnormal (most deficient, excessive, imbalanced, and inversed)[4] meridians (of the twelve meridians) of subject 1 for each group. This analysis examined whether or not any influence between subjects occurred more easily in abnormal meridians.

### 4. *Covariance Analyses for Six Groups with Random Tables*

The computer compiled six different random tables. According to each random table, ten groups of five were made from fifty subjects' application numbers. The covariance analyses were done by assigning X and Y values for each individual of each group to each column of the covariance analyses table.

## D. Analyses and Discussion

### 1. *Six Groups Formed in Order of Application*

#### a. *Group with Application Numbers 1-10*

In the group with application numbers 1-10, the F value for $(L+R)/2$ and $L-R=D$ is more than 1.0 in the heart and gall bladder meridians, but less than 1.0 in the other meridians. $F_{.05}=1.99$, df $n_1=9$, $n_2=80$ at the 5 % significance level. No F value in this group arrives at the 5 % significance level, and it cannot be stated that any change occurred due to the mutual influence of Ki between subjects 1 and 2.

*b. Group with Application Numbers 11-20*

In the group with application numbers 11-20, the F value for (L+R)/2 is 1.96 in the large intestine meridian, indicating that significant influence of Ki occurred at almost the 5% significance level. Table V -2, made to examine the nature of the change, shows that the value of the test measurements (ten measurements performed during the test period), are all lower than the corresponding values for control measurements (ten measurements performed during the control period). Therefore, it can be surmised that the function and Ki of the large intestine meridian was lowered by the mutual influence of Ki between subjects 1 and 2.

**Table V - 2:**
Group with Application
Numbers 11-20
L. Intestine m. (L+R)/2

| | Y | | X |
|---|---|---|---|
| G 1 : | 1653 | $<$ | 1659 |
| G 2 : | 1647 | $<$ | 1657 |
| G 3 : | 1649 | $<$ | 1669 |
| G 4 : | 1648 | $<$ | 1673 |
| G 5 : | 1645 | $<$ | 1659 |
| G 6 : | 1632 | $<$ | 1660 |
| G 7 : | 1633 | $<$ | 1661 |
| G 8 : | 1621 | $<$ | 1680 |
| G 9 : | 1627 | $<$ | 1683 |
| G10 : | 1569 | $<$ | 1688 |

**Table V - 3:**
Group with Application
Numbers 45-51
Liver m. (L+R)/2

| | Y | | X |
|---|---|---|---|
| G 1 : | 2016 | $<$ | 2127 |
| G 2 : | 2016 | $<$ | 2133 |
| G 3 : | 1998 | $<$ | 2110 |
| G 4 : | 1996 | $<$ | 2088 |
| G 5 : | 1993 | $<$ | 2059 |
| G 6 : | 1996 | $<$ | 2079 |
| G 7 : | 1983 | $<$ | 2072 |
| G 8 : | 1998 | $<$ | 2054 |
| G 9 : | 1987 | $<$ | 2046 |
| G10 : | 1981 | $<$ | 2037 |

*c. Group with Application Numbers 21-30*

In the group with application numbers 21-30, the F value for (L+R)/2 of the triple heater meridian is 1.33, but does not arrive at the 5 % significance level.

*d. Group with Application Numbers 31-41*[5]

In the group with application numbers 31-41, the F value

for (L + R)/2 of the spleen meridian is 1.67 and the F value for L − R = D of the stomach branch meridian is 1.43, both of which are larger than one but do not arrive at the 5 % significance level.

*e. Group with Application Numbers 42-51*

In the group with application numbers 42-51, the F value for L − R = D of the large intestine meridian is 1.67 and that of the stomach branch meridian is 1.61. The F value for (L + R)/2 of the liver meridian is 1.92 (close to the 5 % significance level) while that of the urinary bladder meridian is 1.36. The nature of the change in the liver meridian was examined in Table Ⅴ-3. The value for each test measurement is lower than the corresponding value of the control measurement. It can therefore be surmised that the function and Ki of the liver meridian was lowered by the mutual influence of Ki between subjects 1 and 2.

*f. Group with Application Numbers 52-60*

| | Y | | X |
|---|---|---|---|
| G 1 : | 211 | < | 281 |
| G 2 : | 232 | < | 242 |
| G 3 : | 227 | < | 232 |
| G 4 : | 249 | > | 196 |
| G 5 : | 198 | < | 227 |
| G 6 : | 213 | < | 244 |
| G 7 : | 211 | = | 211 |
| G 8 : | 227 | > | 199 |
| G 9 : | 205 | < | 229 |
| G10 : | 195 | < | 228 |
| | 2168 | < | 2289 |

**Table Ⅴ − 4**:
Group with Application Numbers 52 − 60
G. Bladder m. L − R = D

In the group with application numbers 52-60, the F value for (L + R)/2 of the gall bladder meridian is 1.09, and that for L − R = D of this meridian, $F = 2.10 > F_{.05} = 1.99$, df $n_1 = 9$, $n_2 = 80$. That is, a significant change occurred in the D value of the gall bladder meridian of subject 1 by the influence of Ki from subject 2. The nature of this change is listed in Table Ⅴ-4. The sum of the values of each run of the test measurement is smaller than that of the control group measurement. Therefore it can be surmised that the imbalance of the left/right branches of the gall bladder meridian was diminished by the mutual influence of Ki between subjects 1 and 2.

g. *Summary of 1.*

Due to the mutual influence of Ki between the subjects:

* The function and Ki of the large intestine meridian was significantly lowered in the group with application numbers 11-20.
* The function and Ki of the liver meridian was lowered almost at the 5% significance level in the group with application numbers 42-51.
* The imbalance of function and Ki of the right-left branches of the gall bladder meridian was significantly diminished and was more balanced in the group with application numbers 52-60.

In two of the six groups, one group of ten subjects in order of application, the significant change at 5 % was only recorded in one of the twelve meridians for each of these two groups. Therefore it can be surmised that the change in function and Ki, due to the mutual influence of Ki between subjects, is very small.

One possible explanation : In the experimental arrangement where the same pairs of subjects were used as subjects 1 and 2 by turns (see explanation in B.), the mutual influence of Ki might have already taken place in the second experiment and this may account for the small number of significant changes for the entire experiment.

### 2. Normal Meridians

The data of three groups with application numbers 1-10, 11-20, and 21-30 in the six groups were examined to check whether or not the three meridians with normal functioning among the twelve meridians were significantly influenced by mutual influence between subjects.

*a. Group with Application Numbers 1-10*

No significant influence was monitored in the three normal meridians in this group.

*b. Group with Application Numbers 11-20*

No significant influence was monitored in the three normal meridians in this group.

*c. Group with Application Numbers 21-30*

No significant influence was monitored in the three normal meridians in this group.

### *3. Abnormal Meridians*

The data of the group with application numbers 11-20 was examined to check whether or not the four abnormal meridians (whose functional condition was most deficient, excessive, imbalanced and inversed among the twelve meridians) were significantly influenced by the interaction between subjects.

*a. $(L+R)/2$ of the Most Deficient Meridian*

The F value for $(L+R)/2$ of the most deficient meridian is 0.99. This value is insignificant.

*b. $L-R=D$ of the Most Deficient Meridian*

The F value for D of the most deficient meridian is 0.56. This value is insignificant.

*c. $(L+R)/2$ of the Most Excessive Meridian*

The value for $(L+R)/2$ of the most excessive meridian is 0.59. This value is insignificant.

*d. $L-R=D$ of the Most Excessive Meridian*

The F value for D of the most excessive meridian is 0.89. This value is insignificant.

*e. $(L+R)/2$ of the Most Inversed Meridian*

The F value for (L+R)/2 of the most inversed meridian is 0.26. This value is insignificant.

*f. L−R=D of the Most Inversed Meridian*

The F value for D of the most inversed meridian is 0.66. This value is insignificant.

*g. (L+R)/2 of the Most Imbalanced Meridian*

The F value for (L+R)/2 of the most imbalanced meridian is 1.03. Although this reading is higher than 1.0 it does not arrive at the level of significance.

*h. L−R=D for the Most Imbalanced Meridian*

The value for D of the most imbalanced meridian is 0.71. This value is insignificant.

***4. Covariance Analyses for the Groups with Odd Numbers and Those with Even Numbers***

Analyses to determine whether or not significant changes occurred by the mutual influence of Ki in the meridians with normal function in three groups with application numbers 1-10, 11-20, and 21-30 revealed that there had been no significant change. The analyses to determine whether or not significant changes occurred in the meridians with abnormal function, examining the group with application numbers 11-20, had the same result.

The sixty subjects were then divided into two sections with odd and even application nubmers. Each of the sections consisted of three groups (ten subjects per group), and the covariance analyses were performed respectively for each.

The reason for these anlyses was as follows: In this experimental arrangement, the subject with an odd application number formed a pair with the subject with the following even application number. The subject with an odd number was first monitored as subject 1 for the control measurements, then the subject with the even number entered as subject 2. Five minutes later, the subject with the odd number (subject 1) was monitored again for test measurements. During the second experiment, the subject with the even number was monitored as subject 1 for control measurements. The Ki of the subject with the even application number had already received the influence of the subject with the odd number in the first experiment, however, and thus the subject's meridian function had already been changed. Therefore, an identical pattern of meridian functional change may have been produced between a pair of subjects when the subject with the odd number entered the room as subject 2 for the second experiment. In this connection, it can be expected that there may have been fewer significant changes between the control and test data. Contrary to this expectation, more significant changes are expected to have taken place in the first experiment where the subjects with odd numbers were monitored as subject 1 as there had been no mutual influence between this pair of subjects.

To summarize, sixty subjects were divided into two sections with odd and even application numbers. Each section consisted of three groups. The covariance analyses were then performed on each section to examine whether or not significant changes had occcurred in each pair from the mutual influence of Ki in the three normal and four abnormal meridians.

*a. Groups with Odd Numbers*

*i. Normal Meridians*

*Group with Application Numbers 1-19*

No significant changes in the three normal meridians.

*Group with Application Numbers 21-39*

In $L-R=D$ of the third most normal meridian, a significant change was recorded by the mutual influence of Ki at $F=2.61 > F_{.05}=1.99$.

*Group with Application Numbers 41-57*

F values exceeding one were recorded in $L-R=D$ in the second most normal meridian and in $(L+R)/2$ and

L − R = D of the third most normal meridian, but they do not arrive at the 5 % significance level.

ii. *Abnormal Meridians*

*Group with Application Numbers 1-10*

No significant change in the four abnormal meridians.

*Group with Application Numbers 21-39*

No significant change in the four abnormal meridians.

*Group with Application Numbers 41-57*

The F value for (L + R)/2 of the most excessive meridian is 1.35 (exceeding 1.0), but it does not arrive at the 5% significance level. No significant change in the other abnormal meridians.

b. *Groups with Even Numbers*

i. *Normal Meridians*

*Group with Application Numbers 2-20*

No significant change.

*Group with Application Numbers 22-42*

The F value for L − R = D of the third most normal meridian is 1.43 (exceeding 1.0) but does not arrive at the 5 % significance level. No significant changes in other normal meridians.

*Group with Application Numbers 44-60*

No significant change.

ii. *Abnormal Meridians*

*Group with Application Numbers 2-20*

The F value for (L + R)/2 of the most excessive meridian is 1.29 (exceeding 1.0) but does not arrive at the 5 % significance level. The F value for (L + R)/2 and L − R = D for the most imbalanced meridian exceeds one, but does not arrive at the 5 % significance level. There is no significant change in other abnormal meridians.

*Group with Application Numbers 22-42*

The F value for L − R = D of the most deficient meridian is 1.13 (exceeding 1.0) but does not arrive at the 5 %

significance level. There is no significant change in other meridians.

Group with Application Numbers 44-60

No significant change.

### 5. *Observations on the Basis of 2.- 4. of This Section*

*a. Groups Formed in Order of Application*

The covariance analyses which were performed on six groups formed in order of application did not show any significant change in the normal and abnormal meridians.

*b. Groups with Odd Application Numbers and Even Application Numbers*

*i. Normal Meridians*

A significant change was observed at a significance level higher than 5 % in one of the odd numbered groups. No significant change was observed in the even numbered groups.

*ii. Abnormal Meridians*

No significant change was observed in either the odd or even numbered groups.

From the above, it can be said that the frequency of significant change, occurring in the normal/abnormal meridians, is very small in the three groups formed in order of application, and in each of the three groups with odd and even numbers. Only one of the three normal meridians in one of the three odd numbered groups showed a significant change.

Thus, the normality or abnormality of the meridian is not necessarily connected to their susceptibility to the mutual influence of Ki between subjects. However, it can be said that the normal meridians may be to a slight degree more easily influenced by Ki than are the abnormal meridians.

## 6. *Covariance Analyses of Six Groups Formed by Random Tables and Their Results*

Covariance analyses were performed to examine whether or not there were significant changes occurring by the mutual influence of Ki in the six groups (fifty subjects for each group) formed according to six different random tables.

### *a. Group by Random Table 1*

**Table V - 5:**
Group by Random Table 1
G. Bladder m. L − R = D

| | Y | | X |
|---|---|---|---|
| G 1 : | 318 | > | 262 |
| G 2 : | 261 | < | 262 |
| G 3 : | 154 | > | 153 |
| G 4 : | 196 | > | 154 |
| G 5 : | 189 | < | 220 |
| G 6 : | 146 | < | 160 |
| G 7 : | 155 | < | 213 |
| G 8 : | 181 | < | 200 |
| G 9 : | 201 | < | 268 |
| G10 : | 237 | > | 168 |
| | 2038 | < | 2060 |

**Table V - 6:**
Group by Random Table 2
Spleen m. (L + R)/2

| | Y | | X |
|---|---|---|---|
| G 1 : | 2049 | < | 2182 |
| G 2 : | 1842 | < | 1894 |
| G 3 : | 2042 | < | 2074 |
| G 4 : | 1966 | < | 2043 |
| G 5 : | 1886 | < | 2029 |
| G 6 : | 1805 | < | 1876 |
| G 7 : | 2112 | > | 2105 |
| G 8 : | 2022 | < | 2133 |
| G 9 : | 1916 | < | 1959 |
| G10 : | 2083 | < | 2129 |

The F value for L − R = D of the gall bladder meridian is nearing the 5 % significance level ($F = 1.87 \fallingdotseq F_{.05} = 2.12$, $n_1 = 9$, $n_2 = 40$), but does not arrive at 5 % significance. The nature of this change is listed in Table V -5.

The longitudinal numbers 1-10 in Table V -5 indicated the order of measurements of control and test data. The values in the Y column indicate the average value of test data of the five subjects at each measurement, i.e. the value in the Y column at the level of '1' is the average value of the five subjects at the first test measurement.

The values in the X column indicate the average value of the control data of the five subjects at each measurement, i.e. the value in the X column at the level of '1' is the average value of the five subjects at the first control measurement.

When the average of each test data is compared with

the average of the corresponding control data, the average of the test data is larger than that of the corresponding control data in the first, third, fourth, and tenth measurements, but is smaller than that of the corresponding control data in the other six measurements. When the total test data average and control data average are compared, the test data average is smaller. Therefore it can be surmised that the difference of the left-right branches (imbalance) of the gall bladder meridian was decreased by the mutual influence of Ki.

*b. Group by Random Table 2*

The F value is greater than 1.0 in $(L+R)/2$ and/or $L-R=D$ of many meridians in this group. $F=2.28>F_{.05}=2.12$ in $(L+R)/2$ of the spleen meridian; $F=2.08 \fallingdotseq F_{.05}=2.12$ in $L-R=D$ of the stomach meridian; $F=1.91 \fallingdotseq F_{.05}=2.12$ in the $(L+R)/2$ of the kidney meridian.

The nature of the change is as follows: In the $(L+R)/2$ of the spleen meridian, the average of the test data (column Y) is smaller than that of the corresponding control data (column X) in nine of ten measurements, except in the seventh measurement (Table V-6). It can thus be surmised that the meridian function and Ki of the spleen meridian decreased from the mutual influence of Ki.

The total of the averages of the test data is 1337, and that of the control data is 1378 in $L-R=D$ of the stomach meridian. Therefore, it can be surmised that the imbalance between the left and right branches of the stomach meridian decreased from the influence of Ki (Table V-7).

The average of the test data is smaller than that of the corresponding control data in all ten measurments in $(L+R)/2$ of the kidney meridian (Table V-8). This also seems to indicate that the function and Ki of the kidney meridian decreased from the mutual influence of Ki.

*c. Group by Random Table 3*

The F value is more than one in many of the meridians

**Table V − 7**:
Group by Random Table 2
Stomach m. L−R=D

| | Y | | X |
|---|---|---|---|
| G 1 : | 388 | > | 300 |
| G 2 : | 79 | > | 38 |
| G 3 : | 72 | < | 160 |
| G 4 : | 134 | < | 138 |
| G 5 : | 122 | < | 163 |
| G 6 : | 107 | < | 122 |
| G 7 : | 124 | < | 137 |
| G 8 : | 151 | > | 136 |
| G 9 : | 111 | < | 116 |
| G10 : | 49 | < | 68 |
| | 1337 | < | 1378 |

**Table V − 8**:
Group by Random Table 2
Kidney m. (L+R)/2

| | Y | | X |
|---|---|---|---|
| G 1 : | 1641 | < | 1747 |
| G 2 : | 1484 | < | 1532 |
| G 3 : | 1573 | < | 1616 |
| G 4 : | 1731 | < | 1772 |
| G 5 : | 1632 | < | 1715 |
| G 6 : | 1605 | < | 1633 |
| G 7 : | 1643 | < | 1689 |
| G 8 : | 1587 | < | 1721 |
| G 9 : | 1574 | < | 1621 |
| G10 : | 1627 | < | 1726 |

in this group. $F=2.50>F_{.05}=2.12$ in L−R=D of the small intestine meridian, and $F=2.40>F_{.05}=2.12$ in the (L+R)/2 of the urinary bladder meridian. Both of these figures indicate a significant change at the 5 % significance level.

The nature of the change is as follows: The total of the averages of the test data is 1131, and that of the control data is 1171 in L−R=D of the small intestine meridian (Table V-9). Therefore, the imbalance of the function and Ki between the left and right branches of the small intestine meridian decreased as a whole by the mutual influence of Ki. The average of the test data is smaller than that of

**Table V − 9**:
Group by Random Table 3
S. Intestine m. L−R=D

| | Y | | X |
|---|---|---|---|
| G 1 : | 100 | < | 154 |
| G 2 : | 44 | < | 74 |
| G 3 : | 87 | < | 155 |
| G 4 : | 164 | > | 141 |
| G 5 : | 107 | < | 169 |
| G 6 : | 99 | > | 73 |
| G 7 : | 111 | > | 104 |
| G 8 : | 218 | > | 154 |
| G 9 : | 82 | > | 76 |
| G10 : | 119 | > | 71 |
| | 1131 | < | 1171 |

**Table V − 10**:
Group by Random Table 3
U. Bladder m. (L+R)/2

| | Y | | X |
|---|---|---|---|
| G 1 : | 1526 | < | 1605 |
| G 2 : | 1499 | < | 1574 |
| G 3 : | 1778 | < | 1912 |
| G 4 : | 1567 | < | 1594 |
| G 5 : | 1532 | < | 1582 |
| G 6 : | 1548 | < | 1564 |
| G 7 : | 1743 | < | 1789 |
| G 8 : | 1766 | < | 1827 |
| G 9 : | 1542 | < | 1580 |
| G10 : | 1420 | < | 1449 |

the corresponding control data in all the measurements in (L+R)/2 of the urinary bladder meridian (Table Ⅴ-10). Therefore the function and Ki of the urinary bladder meridian was decreased by the mutual influence of Ki.

*d. Group by Randon Table 4*

**Table Ⅴ - 11**: Group by Random Table 4 G. Bladder m. (L+R)/2

| | Y | | X |
|---|---|---|---|
| G 1 : | 1595 | < | 1612 |
| G 2 : | 1678 | < | 1750 |
| G 3 : | 1525 | < | 1630 |
| G 4 : | 1438 | < | 1523 |
| G 5 : | 1539 | < | 1583 |
| G 6 : | 1618 | < | 1702 |
| G 7 : | 1441 | < | 1453 |
| G 8 : | 1717 | < | 1768 |
| G 9 : | 1448 | < | 1466 |
| G10 : | 1661 | < | 1662 |

**Table Ⅴ - 12**: Group by Random Table 4 U. Bladder m. (L+R)/2

| | Y | | X |
|---|---|---|---|
| G 1 : | 1548 | < | 1630 |
| G 2 : | 1648 | < | 1688 |
| G 3 : | 1630 | < | 1732 |
| G 4 : | 1594 | < | 1677 |
| G 5 : | 1455 | < | 1501 |
| G 6 : | 1416 | < | 1441 |
| G 7 : | 1541 | < | 1571 |
| G 8 : | 1766 | < | 1850 |
| G 9 : | 1568 | < | 1584 |
| G10 : | 1872 | < | 1904 |

The F value is larger than 1.0 in many of the meridians in this group. $F=3.08>F_{.01}=2.88$ for (L+R)/2 of the gall bladder meridian indicates a significant change at the 1 % significance level. $F=2.06 \fallingdotseq F_{.05}=2.12$ for (L+R)/2 of the urinary bladder meridian indicates a significant change at the level nearing 5 % significance. The nature of these changes are listed in Tables Ⅴ-11 and Ⅴ-12. The average of the test data is smaller than that of the corresponding control data in all ten measurements in (L+R)/2 for both the gall bladder meridian and the urinary bladder meridians. Therefore it can be said that the function and Ki of the gall bladder and urinary bladder meridians were decreased by the mutual influence of Ki.

*e. Group by Random Table 5*

The F value is more than 1.0 in many of the meridians in this group. $F=2.46>F_{.05}=2.12$ in (L+R)/2 of the lung meridian indicates a significant change at the 5 % level.

The nature of the change is in Table Ⅴ-13 : The average of the test data is smaller than that of the corresponding control data in all ten measurements. It can thus be considered that the function and Ki of the lung meridian was decreased by the mutual influence of Ki.

**Table V - 13**:
Group by Random Table 5
Lung m. (L+R)/2

| | Y | | X |
|---|---|---|---|
| G 1 : | 2132 | < | 2292 |
| G 2 : | 2092 | < | 2179 |
| G 3 : | 2082 | < | 2115 |
| G 4 : | 1995 | < | 2105 |
| G 5 : | 1966 | < | 2076 |
| G 6 : | 2066 | < | 2225 |
| G 7 : | 2072 | < | 2242 |
| G 8 : | 1938 | < | 2022 |
| G 9 : | 2147 | < | 2180 |
| G10 : | 1950 | < | 2030 |

**Table V - 14**:
Group by Random Table 6
Lung m. (L+R)/2

| | Y | | X |
|---|---|---|---|
| G 1 : | 1921 | < | 1991 |
| G 2 : | 1954 | < | 2026 |
| G 3 : | 1975 | < | 2074 |
| G 4 : | 2165 | < | 2188 |
| G 5 : | 2011 | < | 2088 |
| G 6 : | 1957 | < | 2148 |
| G 7 : | 1968 | < | 2108 |
| G 8 : | 1998 | < | 2063 |
| G 9 : | 1986 | < | 2102 |
| G10 : | 2203 | < | 2321 |

*f. Group by Random Table 6*

The F value is larger than one in many of the meridians in this group. $F=2.31>F_{.05}=2.12$ in $(L+R)/2$ of the lung meridian ; $F=2.77>F_{.05}=2.12$ in $(L+R)/2$ of the spleen meridian ; $F=2.23>F_{.05}=2.12$ in $L-R=D$ of the gall bladder meridian, all of which indicate a significant change at the 5 % significance level.

The nature of the change is as follows : The average of the test data is smaller than that of the corresponding control data in all the measurements in $(L+R)/2$ of the lung meridian. It can be concluded that the function and Ki of the lung meridian decreased due to the mutual influence of Ki (Table Ⅴ-14).

The average of the test data is smaller than that of the corresponding control data average in nine of ten measurements in $(L+R)/2$ of the spleen meridian. The exception is found in the sixth measurement. It can be concluded that the function and Ki of the spleen meridian decreased from the mutual influence of Ki (Table Ⅴ-15).

The average of the test data is smaller than that of the

corresponding control data in nine of ten measurements in L − R = D of the gall bladder meridian. The exception is found to be the sixth measurement. Therefore it can be concluded that the imbalance between the left and right branches of the gall bladder meridian was decreased by the mutual influence of Ki (Table V-16).

**Table V − 15**:
Group by Random Table 6
Spleen m. (L+R)/2

| | Y | | X |
|---|---|---|---|
| G 1 : | 1937 | < | 1973 |
| G 2 : | 1924 | < | 2012 |
| G 3 : | 2023 | < | 2140 |
| G 4 : | 2104 | < | 2208 |
| G 5 : | 1874 | < | 1946 |
| G 6 : | 2242 | > | 2234 |
| G 7 : | 2010 | < | 2114 |
| G 8 : | 1663 | < | 1823 |
| G 9 : | 1950 | < | 2032 |
| G10 : | 1924 | < | 2024 |

**Table V − 16**:
Group by Random Table 6
G. Bladder m. L − R = D

| | Y | | X |
|---|---|---|---|
| G 1 : | 73 | < | 110 |
| G 2 : | 208 | < | 227 |
| G 3 : | 182 | < | 243 |
| G 4 : | 179 | < | 238 |
| G 5 : | 267 | < | 317 |
| G 6 : | 352 | > | 281 |
| G 7 : | 204 | < | 244 |
| G 8 : | 148 | < | 152 |
| G 9 : | 177 | < | 218 |
| G10 : | 202 | < | 231 |

*g. Discussion and Considerations*

*i. Meridians Which Showed Significant Changes*

The meridians which showed significant changes at more than the 5 % significance level in six groups formed by random tables are as follows :

| | | |
|---|---|---|
| G. bladder meridian | (L+R)/2 | the 4th Group |
| | L − R = D | the 6th Group |
| Spleen meridian | (L+R)/2 | the 2nd & 6th Groups |
| Stomach meridian | L − R = D | the 2nd Group |
| Kidney meridian | (L+R)/2 | the 2nd Group |
| S. intestine meridian | L − R = D | the 3rd Group |
| U. bladder meridian | (L+R)/2 | the 3rd & 4th Groups |
| Lung meridian | (L+R)/2 | the 5th & 6th Groups |

A total of eleven meridians showed significant changes in the six groups. Compared with the significant change in a total of two meridians in the examination of the six groups (each comprised of ten subjects in order of application), more meridians showed significant changes. In the former analyses of groups formed in order of application, the data of ten measurements for the same ten subjects was classified by the 1st (G1) to the tenth (G10) measurement. Contrary to this classification, each of the latter ten measurements (G) includes the data of five different subjects examined in the analyses of fifty subjects with random tables. Using this arrangment, each group may be equal in the ability to receive Ki influence; and as a result, the mutual influence of Ki seems to have been more clearly shown in the covariance analyses.

*ii. Nature of Change*

* In the group listed under random table 2, both the function and Ki of the spleen and kidney meridians, and the imbalance of the left-right branches of the stomach meridian decreased.
* In the group listed under random table 3, the function and Ki of the urinary bladder meridian, and the imbalance of the left-right branches of the small intestine meridian decreased.
* In the group listed under random table 4, the function and Ki of the gall bladder and urinary bladder meridians decreased.
* In the group listed under random table 5, the function and Ki of the lung meridian decreased.
* In the group listed under random table 6, the function and Ki of the lung and spleen meridians, and the imbalance of the left-right branches of the gall bladder meridian decreased.

*iii. Summary*

In the total eleven meridians which showed significant changes by the mutual influence of Ki, function and Ki decreased in all the meridians which showed significant changes in $(L+R)/2$, and imbalance of the left-right branches decreased, that is, left/right balance was restored in all the meridians which showed significant changes in L − R = D. These features are common to the nature of the change.

Next, the meridians which showed significant changes were classified according to both body systems and corresponding Chakra systems:

* The gall bladder, spleen and stomach meridians distribute Ki and are closely related to the digestive system (Manipura Chakra).
* The kidney and urinary bladder meridians distribute Ki and are closely related to the urogenital system (Svadhishthana Chakra).
* The small intestine meridian distributes Ki and is related to the pituitary gland (Ajna Chakra) and circulatory system (Anahata Chakra).
* The lung meridian distributes Ki and is closely related to the respiratory system (Vishuddhi Chakra).

In Yogic tradition it has been empirically known that the Manipura Chakra (which is related to the digestive system) is the foremost receptor of Prana or Ki. Therefore the fact that five of the eleven meridians which showed significant changes are related to the digestive system (Manipura Chakra) seems indicative of both the empirical knowledge of ancient religious experiences and experimental evidence.

### 7. T-test and $x^2$ Test Analyses of Ki Influence on the Meridian Functions of Others

As was explained in section B (Experimental Procedure) ten AMI measurements were taken during the control period. In the test period a second set of ten measurements was taken. The average of (L + R)/2 and that of L − R = D of both sets of measurements were calculated for each meridian of each individual. Changes were expected to have occurred in the function and Ki of subject 1's meridians by the mutual influence of Ki between subjects. T-tests were then performed for (L + R)/2 and L − R = D of each meridian of each subject in order to examine whether or not any significant difference between the corresponding averages existed;

that is, whether or not any significant change occurred from the mutual influence of Ki. For each group formed in order of application, the number of meridians showing significant change in each subject in the above t-tests was totaled respectively for (L+R)/2 and L−R=D for each meridian. In the same manner, the totals of the meridians in each subject which did not show any significant change were calculated respectively for (L+R)/2 and L−R=D. $x^2$ tests were then performed to examine whether or not any significant difference existed among the twelve meridians ; that is, which meridians were significantly influenced. Furthermore, to examine whether or not any significant difference existed between the frequency of significant and insignificant changes for each meridian (which meridians were more frequently influenced) $x^2$ tests were performed for the rate of change 〔(frequency of significant change/frequency of insignificant change)×100〕 of each meridian without separating (L+R)/2 and L−R=D, and the same $x^2$ tests were also performed respectively for (L+R)/2 and L−R=D.

*a. Group with Application Numbers 1-10*

**Table V − 17-1**

〔(L+R)/2, | L−R |〕

| | LU | LI | HC | TH | HT | SI | SP | LV | ST | GB | KI | UB |
|---|---|---|---|---|---|---|---|---|---|---|---|---|
| N | 5 | 5 | 15 | 10 | 8 | 8 | 9 | 6 | 11 | 5 | 8 | 10 |
| C | 15 | 15 | 5 | 10 | 12 | 12 | 11 | 14 | 9 | 15 | 12 | 10 |

( $\chi 2$ =19.89 > $\chi 2$ (r =.05)=19.68 df=11 )

Notes for tables : N = Frequency of no significant change
C = Frequency of significant change

**Table V − 17-2**

〔(L+R)/2, | L−R |〕

| | LU | LI | HC | TH | HT | SI | SP | LV | ST | GB | KI | UB |
|---|---|---|---|---|---|---|---|---|---|---|---|---|
| % | 300.0 | 300.0 | 33.3 | 100.0 | 150.0 | 150.0 | 122.2 | 233.3 | 81.8 | 300.0 | 150.0 | 100.0 |

( $\chi 2$ =560.69 > $\chi 2$ (r =.01)=24.72 df=11,
%=frequency of significant change / that of insignificant)

*i.* In $x^2$ tests performed for the sum frequencies of (L+R)/2 and L−R=D, $x^2=19.89>x^2_{.05}=19.68$. This result shows a significant difference between the frequency distribution of significant and insignificant changes for each meridian at the 5 % significance level. In Table V-17-1, the meridians which showed a higher frequency of significant change than the average frequency of significant change (11.7), which is derived by dividing the sum total of frequencies of significant change of each meridian by twelve (twelve meridians), were the lung, large intestine, gall bladder, liver, kidney, heart, and small intestine meridians. In $x^2$ tests for the rates of significant change in Table V-17-2, the same tendency was indicated at a 1 % significance level.

*ii.* In $x^2$ tests for (L+R)/2, $x^2=16.19<x^2_{.05}=19.68$. In $x^2$ tests for L−R=D, $x^2=17.41<x^2_{.05}=19.68$, both of which fall slightly short of the 5 % significance level.

*iii.* The significant changes of each meridian which showed higher frequency than the average in the above $x^2$ tests table for the sum frequencies of (L+R)/2 and L−R=D were divided into the categories of frequency towards increase and frequency towards decrease. Further, $x^2$ tests were performed to examine whether the nature of the change of each meridian is towards increase or decrease respectively for (L+R)/2 and L−R=D (Table V-18-1, 18-2).

In Table V-18-1 the lung, liver, gall bladder and kidney meridians showed decrease of function and Ki at the 5 % significance level. Although the values for the large intestine, heart and small intestine meridians were slightly less than the 5 % significance level, they similarly displayed a tendency to decrease.

In Table V-18-2 significant increase in imbalance between the left-right branches was recorded in the large intestine meridian, but there was no significant difference in L−R=D in the other six meridians.

## Table V − 18-1

〔(L+R)/2〕 BP

| | LU | LI | HC | TH | HT | SI | SP | LV | ST | GB | KI | UB | Sum |
|---|---|---|---|---|---|---|---|---|---|---|---|---|---|
| N | 1 | 3 | 7 | 5 | 3 | 3 | 1 | 2 | 3 | 1 | 4 | 3 | 36 |
| C | 9 | 7 | 3 | 5 | 7 | 7 | 9 | 8 | 7 | 9 | 6 | 7 | 84 |
| D | 8 | 6 | 2 | 5 | 6 | 6 | 6 | 8 | 6 | 8 | 6 | 7 | 74 |
| I | 1 | 1 | 1 | 0 | 1 | 1 | 3 | 0 | 1 | 1 | 0 | 0 | 10 |

| | LU | LI | HC | TH | HT | SI | SP | LV | ST | GB | KI | UB | Sum |
|---|---|---|---|---|---|---|---|---|---|---|---|---|---|
| SD | SD | | — | — | | | | SD | | SD | SD | SD | — |
| X | 5.4 | 3.6 | 0.0 | 0.0 | 3.6 | 3.6 | 1.0 | 8.0 | 3.6 | 5.4 | 6.0 | 7.0 | — |
| % | 0.025 | 0.050 | 0.000 | 0.000 | 0.050 | 0.050 | 0.050 | 0.005 | 0.050 | 0.025 | 0.025 | 0.010 | — |
| x | 5.0 | 3.8 | 0.0 | 0.0 | 3.8 | 3.8 | 3.8 | 7.9 | 3.8 | 5.0 | 5.0 | 6.6 | — |

| | LU | LI | HC | TH | HT | SI | SP | LV | ST | GB | KI | UB | Sum |
|---|---|---|---|---|---|---|---|---|---|---|---|---|---|
| D | D | | | | | | | D | | D | D | D | — |
| I | | | | | | | | | | | | | — |

Notes for tables :
N = Frequency of no significant change
C = Frequency of significant change
D = Decrease
I = Increase
SD = Significant difference
X = $\chi 2$ test value
% = Closest significance level to the above $\chi 2$ test value
x = Value of the above significance level

## Table V − 18-2

〔| L−R |〕 BP

| | LU | LI | HC | TH | HT | SI | SP | LV | ST | GB | KI | UB | Sum |
|---|---|---|---|---|---|---|---|---|---|---|---|---|---|
| N | 4 | 2 | 8 | 5 | 5 | 5 | 8 | 4 | 8 | 4 | 4 | 7 | 64 |
| C | 6 | 8 | 2 | 5 | 5 | 5 | 2 | 6 | 2 | 6 | 6 | 3 | 56 |
| D | 1 | 1 | 2 | 5 | 3 | 3 | 1 | 4 | 1 | 3 | 4 | 3 | 31 |
| I | 5 | 7 | 0 | 0 | 2 | 2 | 1 | 2 | 1 | 3 | 2 | 0 | 25 |

| | LU | LI | HC | TH | HT | SI | SP | LV | ST | GB | KI | UB | Sum |
|---|---|---|---|---|---|---|---|---|---|---|---|---|---|
| SD | | SD | — | — | — | — | — | | — | — | | — | — |
| X | 2.7 | 4.5 | 0.0 | 0.0 | 0.0 | 0.0 | 0.0 | 0.7 | 0.0 | 0.0 | 0.7 | 0.0 | — |
| % | 0.050 | 0.050 | 0.000 | 0.000 | 0.000 | 0.000 | 0.000 | 0.050 | 0.000 | 0.000 | 0.050 | 0.000 | — |
| x | 3.8 | 3.8 | 0.0 | 0.0 | 0.0 | 0.0 | 0.0 | 3.8 | 0.0 | 0.0 | 3.8 | 0.0 | — |

| | LU | LI | HC | TH | HT | SI | SP | LV | ST | GB | KI | UB | Sum |
|---|---|---|---|---|---|---|---|---|---|---|---|---|---|
| D | | | | | | | | | | | | | — |
| I | | I | | | | | | | | | | | — |

*b. Group with Application Numbers 11-20*

In the $\chi^2$ test for the sum frequency of (L+R)/2 and L−R=D, $\chi^2=8.97<\chi^2_{.05}=19.68$, which reveals no significant difference between the frequency distribution of significant and insignificant changes.

Similarly, no significant difference was found in the $\chi^2$ test for (L+R)/2 or the $\chi^2$ test for L−R=D.

*c. Group with Application Numbers 21-30*

In the $\chi^2$ test for the sum frequencies of (L+R)/2 and L−R=D, $\chi^2=12.10>\chi^2_{.05}=19.68$, which showed no significant difference. For (L+R)/2, $\chi^2=23.60>\chi^2_{.025}=21.92$ showed a significant difference at the 2.5 % significance level. The meridians which showed a higher than average frequency

**Table V − 19**

〔(L+R)/2〕

| | (LU) | LI | HC | (TH) | (HT) | SI | (SP) | (LV) | ST | (GB) | (KI) | (UB) |
|---|---|---|---|---|---|---|---|---|---|---|---|---|
| N | 0 | 4 | 5 | 2 | 0 | 5 | 2 | 0 | 3 | 2 | 0 | 2 |
| C | (10) | 6 | 5 | (8) | (10) | 5 | (8) | (10) | 7 | (8) | (10) | (8) |

($\chi 2=23.60>\chi 2\ (r=.05)=19.68$  df=11)

**Table V − 20**

〔(L+R)/2〕  BP

| | (LU) | LI | HC | (TH) | (HT) | SI | (SP) | (LV) | ST | (GB) | (KI) | (UB) | Sum |
|---|---|---|---|---|---|---|---|---|---|---|---|---|---|
| N | 0 | 4 | 5 | 2 | 0 | 5 | 2 | 0 | 3 | 2 | 0 | 2 | 25 |
| C | 10 | 6 | 5 | 8 | 10 | 5 | 8 | 10 | 7 | 8 | 10 | 8 | 95 |
| D | 10 | 6 | 5 | 7 | 10 | 5 | 8 | 10 | 7 | 6 | 10 | 8 | 92 |
| I | 0 | 0 | 0 | 1 | 0 | 0 | 0 | 0 | 0 | 2 | 0 | 0 | 3 |

| | LU | LI | HC | TH | HT | SI | SP | LV | ST | GB | KI | UB | Sum |
|---|---|---|---|---|---|---|---|---|---|---|---|---|---|
| SD | (SD) | — | — | (SD) | (SD) | — | (SD) | (SD) | SD | | (SD) | (SD) | — |
| X | 10.0 | 0.0 | 0.0 | 4.5 | 10.0 | 0.0 | 8.0 | 10.0 | 7.0 | 2.0 | 10.0 | 8.0 | — |
| % | 0.005 | 0.000 | 0.000 | 0.050 | 0.005 | 0.000 | 0.005 | 0.005 | 0.010 | 0.050 | 0.005 | 0.005 | — |
| x | 7.9 | 0.0 | 0.0 | 3.8 | 7.9 | 0.0 | 7.9 | 7.9 | 6.6 | 3.8 | 7.9 | 7.9 | — |

| | (LU) | LI | HC | (TH) | (HT) | SI | (SP) | (LV) | ST | GB | (KI) | (UB) | Sum |
|---|---|---|---|---|---|---|---|---|---|---|---|---|---|
| D | D | | | D | D | | D | D | D | | D | D | — |
| I | | | | | | | | | | | | | — |

of significant change (7.9) are the lung, triple heater, heart, spleen, liver, gall bladder, kidney, and urinary bladder (Table V-19).

In Table V-20, an examination of the nature of change (toward increase or decrease) reveals that seven meridians showed a significant difference in the decrease of function and Ki. Although the gall bladder meridian did not show a significant difference, its change was also in the direction of decrease.

For L−R=D, $x^2=5.83<x^2_{.05}=19.68$, which shows no significant difference between the frequency distributions of significance and insignificance.

*d. Group with Application Numbers 31-41*

In $x^2$ tests for the sum frequencies of (L+R)/2 and L−R=D, $x^2=17.32<x^2_{.05}=19.68$. $x^2=18.22<x^2_{.05}=19.68$ for (L+R)/2 and $x^2=12.54<x^2_{.05}=19.68$ for L−R=D. None of these frequencies displayed significant change.

*e. Group with Application Numbers 42-51*

**Table V − 21**

〔(L+R)/2〕

| | (LU) | LI | (HC) | TH | HT | SI | (SP) | (LV) | (ST) | (GB) | (KI) | UB |
|---|---|---|---|---|---|---|---|---|---|---|---|---|
| N | 1 | 3 | 2 | 4 | 6 | 3 | 1 | 0 | 0 | 0 | 1 | 3 |
| C | (9) | 7 | (8) | 6 | 4 | 7 | (9) | (10) | (10) | (10) | (9) | 7 |

($\chi 2=23.75>\chi 2$ (r=.05)=19.68 df=11)

In $x^2$ tests performed for the sum frequencies of (L+R)/2 and L−R=D, $x^2=12.23<x^2_{.05}=19.68$ showed no significant change. $x^2=23.75>x^2_{.02}=22.62$ for (L+R)/2 showed a significant change between frequency distributions of significant and insignificant changes at the 2% significance level (Table V-21).

The meridians which showed a higher frequency than eight, which is the average frequency for significant change,

## Table V - 22

〔(L+R)/2〕 BP

| | LU | LI | HC | TH | HT | SI | SP | LV | ST | GB | KI | UB | Sum |
|---|---|---|---|---|---|---|---|---|---|---|---|---|---|
| N | 1 | 3 | 2 | 4 | 6 | 3 | 1 | 0 | 0 | 0 | 1 | 3 | 24 |
| C | 9 | 7 | 8 | 6 | 4 | 7 | 9 | 10 | 10 | 10 | 9 | 7 | 96 |
| D | 8 | 7 | 7 | 6 | 4 | 7 | 8 | 10 | 10 | 10 | 9 | 7 | 93 |
| I | 1 | 0 | 1 | 0 | 0 | 0 | 1 | 0 | 0 | 0 | 0 | 0 | 3 |

| | LU | LI | HC | TH | HT | SI | SP | LV | ST | GB | KI | UB | Sum |
|---|---|---|---|---|---|---|---|---|---|---|---|---|---|
| SD | SD | SD | SD | SD | — | SD | SD | SD | SD | SD | SD | SD | — |
| X | 5. 4 | 7. 0 | 4. 5 | 6. 0 | 0. 0 | 7. 0 | 5. 4 | 10. 0 | 10. 0 | 10. 0 | 9. 0 | 7. 0 | — |
| % | 0. 025 | 0. 010 | 0. 050 | 0. 025 | 0. 000 | 0. 010 | 0. 025 | 0. 005 | 0. 005 | 0. 005 | 0. 005 | 0. 010 | — |
| x | 5. 0 | 6. 6 | 3. 8 | 5. 0 | 0. 0 | 6. 6 | 5. 0 | 7. 9 | 7. 9 | 7. 9 | 7. 9 | 6. 6 | — |

| | LU | LI | HC | TH | HT | SI | SP | LV | ST | GB | KI | UB | Sum |
|---|---|---|---|---|---|---|---|---|---|---|---|---|---|
| D | D | D | D | D | | D | D | D | D | D | D | D | — |
| I | | | | | | | | | | | | | — |

are the lung, heart constrictor, spleen, liver, stomach, gall bladder, and kidney meridians. For all seven, the nature of the change in each meridian reflects significant decrease (Table V-22). $x^2 = 12.14 < x^2_{.05} = 19.68$ for L − R = D does not show any significant difference.

### *f. Group with Application Numbers 52-60*

In $x^2$ tests, performed for the sum frequencies of (L+R)/2 and L − R = D, $x^2 = 12.25 < x^2_{.05} = 19.68$ showed no significant difference.

$x^2 = 19.96 > x^2_{.05} = 19.68$ for (L+R)/2 showed a significant difference at the 5 % significance level. The meridians which

## Table V - 23

〔(L+R)/2〕

| | LU | LI | HC | TH | HT | SI | SP | LV | ST | GB | KI | UB |
|---|---|---|---|---|---|---|---|---|---|---|---|---|
| N | 0 | 0 | 2 | 3 | 4 | 3 | 0 | 0 | 2 | 0 | 1 | 1 |
| C | 9 | 9 | 7 | 6 | 5 | 6 | 9 | 9 | 7 | 9 | 8 | 8 |

($\chi 2 = 19.96 > \chi 2(r = .05) 19.68$ df = 11)

## Table V - 24

〔(L+R)/2〕　BP

| | LU | LI | HC | TH | HT | SI | SP | LV | ST | GB | KI | UB | Sum |
|---|---|---|---|---|---|---|---|---|---|---|---|---|---|
| N | 0 | 0 | 2 | 3 | 4 | 3 | 0 | 0 | 2 | 0 | 1 | 1 | 16 |
| C | 9 | 9 | 7 | 6 | 5 | 6 | 9 | 9 | 7 | 9 | 8 | 8 | 92 |
| D | 9 | 8 | 6 | 6 | 5 | 5 | 9 | 9 | 7 | 9 | 8 | 8 | 89 |
| I | 0 | 1 | 1 | 0 | 0 | 1 | 0 | 0 | 0 | 0 | 0 | 0 | 3 |

| | LU | LI | HC | TH | HT | SI | SP | LV | ST | GB | KI | UB | Sum |
|---|---|---|---|---|---|---|---|---|---|---|---|---|---|
| SD | SD | SD | | SD | — | | SD | SD | SD | SD | SD | SD | — |
| X | 9.0 | 5.4 | 3.6 | 6.0 | 0.0 | 2.7 | 9.0 | 9.0 | 7.0 | 9.0 | 8.0 | 8.0 | — |
| % | 0.005 | 0.025 | 0.050 | 0.025 | 0.000 | 0.050 | 0.005 | 0.005 | 0.010 | 0.005 | 0.005 | 0.005 | — |
| x | 7.9 | 5.0 | 3.8 | 5.0 | 0.0 | 3.8 | 7.9 | 7.9 | 6.6 | 7.9 | 7.9 | 7.9 | — |

| | LU | LI | HC | TH | HT | SI | SP | LV | ST | GB | KI | UB | Sum |
|---|---|---|---|---|---|---|---|---|---|---|---|---|---|
| D | D | D | | D | | | D | D | D | D | D | D | — |
| I | | | | | | | | | | | | | — |

showed a higher frequency than 7.7, the average frequency of significant change, are the lung, large intestine, spleen, liver, gall bladder, kidney, and urinary bladder meridians (Table V-23). The nature of change for these seven meridians reflects a significant decrease of function and Ki (Table V-24). $x^2=9.68<x^2_{.05}=19.68$ for L－R＝D, does not show any significant difference.

### 8. *Discussion and Considerations on Section 7.*

*a.* In the group with application numbers 1-10, the lung, large intestine, gall bladder, liver, kidney, heart and small intestine meridians showed a high frequency of significant change.

*b.* In the group with application numbers 21-30, the lung, triple heater, heart, spleen, liver, gall bladder, kidney and urinary bladder meridians showed a high frequency of significant change.

*c.* In the group with application numbers 42-51, the lung,

Table V - 25

| LU | LI | GB | LV | KI | HT | SI | TH | SP | UB | HC |
|---|---|---|---|---|---|---|---|---|---|---|
| 4 | 2 | 4 | 4 | 4 | 2 | 1 | 1 | 3 | 3 | 1 |

heart constrictor, spleen, liver, stomach, gall bladder, and kidney meridians showed a high frequency of change.

*d.* In the group with application numbers 52-60, the lung, large intestine, spleen, liver, gall bladder, kidney and urinary bladder meridians showed a high frequency of change.

*e.* The frequency of the meridians which showed a high frequency of significant change is summed up in Table V-25. The lung, gall bladder, liver, spleen, kidney, and urinary bladder meridians showed a high frequency of significant change in more than three of the six groups. It can be surmised that these six meridians are the meridians which are more easily influenced by the mutual influence of Ki. These meridians are classified according to the body-Chakra systems :

Lung meridian — Respiratory system (Vishuddhi Chakra)
Gall bladder, liver, spleen meridians — Digestive system (Manipura Chakra)
Kidney and urinary bladder meridians—Urogenital system (Svadhishthana Chakra)

*f.* The nature of change for meridians which showed a high frequency of significant change by the mutual influence of Ki was a decrease of function and Ki, except for an increase of the imbalance of the left-right branches of the large intestine meridian (Table V-26).

**Table V − 26**

| | Group (1-10) | Group (11-20) | Group (42-51) | Group (52-60) |
|---|---|---|---|---|
| LU | D | D | D | D |
| LV | D | D | D | D |
| GB | D | | D | D |
| KI | D | D | D | D |
| LI | Increase of L− R imbalance | | | D |
| HT | | D | | |
| TH | | D | | |
| SP | | D | D | D |
| HC | | | D | |
| ST | | | D | |
| UB | | D | | D |

## E. Control Experiment

In order to examine whether or not any significant change is produced in the meridian function by the mutual influence of Ki between numbers of people, the experiment and analyses described in the previous sections were performed.

To further examine whether these results actually derived from the mutual influence of Ki between subjects, another experiment not having subject 2 enter the room, was performed on 50 subjects. The procedure for this control experiment was as follows : The meridian function of subject 1 was monitored 10 times as control and 10 times after a lapse of 5 minutes, without having subject 2 enter the room. Further analyses and considerations were done with the covariance analyses, t-tests and $x^2$ tests which were performed to examine whether or not any significant change existed in any of the meridians between these control data.

### 1. *Results of the Covariance Analyses*

With six different random tables, six groups (fifty subjects each) were made from the subjects of this control-control experiment. Covariance anlayses were performed to see whether or not any significant functional change occurred in any of the twelve meridians due to time lapse, room temperature change, etc.

#### a. *Group by Random Table 1*

**Table V - 27**

Gall Bladder meridian ; L - R = D
Y (Control 2 ) ; X1 (Control 1 )
AVE 154 159

| | MS | SS | DF | F |
|---|---|---|---|---|
| TOTAL | BG * T(YX) = 0. 459265E + 06 | SO = 0. 228005E + 06 | 48 | |
| ERROR | B * E(yx) = 0. 237677E + 06 | S I = 0. 154777E + 06 | 39 | |
| | | SC = 0. 154777E + 06 | 9 | 2. 050170 |

Notes: Value in Y is the overall average of Control 2 of 50 subjects (10 groups each of which consists of 5 subjects) and value in X1 is the overall average of Control 1 of the same subjects.

$F = 2.05 \fallingdotseq F_{.05} = 2.12$ $n_1 = 9$, $n_2 = 40$ in L - R = D of the gall bladder meridian shows a significant change at the level nearing 5 % significance. As the average of control 1 = 159 and the average of control 2 = 154, the nature of change is a small decrease. That is, this indicates that the imbalance between the right and left branches of the gall bladder meridian decreased slightly along the time lapse and by the influence of room temperature change (Table V -27).

$F = 2.21 > F_{.05} = 2.12$ for L - R = D of the kidney meridian shows a significant change at the 5 % significance level. As the average of control 1 = 147 and that of control 2 = 142, the nature of the change is a small decrease. That is, this indicates that the imbalance between the right and left branches of the kidney meridian decreased along the time lapse and by the influence of room temperature change.

*b. Group by Random Table 2*

$F = 2.36 > F_{.05} = 2.12$ for $L - R = D$ of the triple heater meridian shows significant change at the 5 % significance level. As the average of control 1 is 149 and that of control 2 is 170, the nature of the change is an increase. That is, this indicates that the imbalance between the right and left branches of the triple heater meridian increased along the time lapse and by the influence of room temperature.

*c. Group by Random Table 3*

No significant change in any of the meridians.

*d. Group by Random Table 4*

$F = 2.089 \fallingdotseq F_{.05} = 2.12$ for $L - R = D$ of the gall bladder meridian indicates a significant difference at the level nearing 5 % significance. As the average of control 1 = 158 and that of control 2 = 153, the nature of change is a small decrease. That is, this indicates that the imbalance between the left and right branches of the gall bladder meridian decreased a little along the time lapse and by change in room temperature.

*e. Group by Random Table 5*

$F = 2.26 > F_{.05} = 2.12$ for $L - R = D$ of the heart constrictor meridian shows a significant change at the 5 % significance level. As the average of control 1 = 161 and that of control 2 = 158, the change is a small decrease. That is, the imbalance of the left-right branches of the heart constrictor meridian decreased slightly along the time lapse and due to room temperature change.

$F=2.65>F_{.05}=2.12$ for $L-R=D$ of the small intestine meridian shows a significant change at the 5 % significance level. As the average of control $1=109$ and that of control $2=138$, the nature of the change is a considerable increase. That is, the imbalance of function and Ki between the left and right branches of the small intestine meridian increased considerably along the time lapse and due to room temperature change.

$F=2.01\fallingdotseq F_{.05}=2.12$ for $L-R=D$ of the urinary bladder meridian shows a significant change at the level nearing 5 % significance. As the average of control $1=204$, and that of control $2=193$, the change is a decrease. That is, the imbalance between the left and right branches of the urinary bladder meridian decreased along the time lapse and by the change in room temperature.

*f. Group by Random Table 6*

$F=2.08\fallingdotseq F_{.05}=2.12$ for $(L+R)/2$ of the heart meridian shows a significant change at the level nearing 5 % significance. As the average of control $1=1615$ and that of control $2=1602$, the nature of the change is a decrease. That is, the meridian function and Ki of the heart meridian decreased along the time lapse and by room temperature change.

$F=1.94\fallingdotseq F_{.05}=2.12$ for $(L+R)/2$ of the spleen meridian shows a significant change at the level nearing 5 % significance. As the average of control $1=1857$, and that of control $2=1793$, the nature of the change is a decrease. That is, the function and Ki of the spleen meridian decreased along the time lapse and by the change in room temperature.

$F=2.14>F_{.05}=2.12$ for $L-R=D$ of the liver meridian shows a significant change at the 5 % significance level. The average of control $1=124$ and that of control $2=111$, the nature of the change is a small decrease. That is, the imbalance between the left and right branches of the liver meridian decreased slightly along the time lapse and the influence of the change in room temperature.

## *2. Discussion and Considerations on Section 1.*

**Table V - 28**

| Meridian | (L+R)/2<br>L−R = D | Group | Nature of Change | Chakra |
|---|---|---|---|---|
| GB | L−R = D<br>L−R = D | Group 1<br>Group 4 | Decrease<br>Decrease | Manipura |
| KI | L−R = D | Group 1 | Decrease | Svadhishthana |
| TH | L−R = D | Group 2 | Increase | Anahata |
| HC | L−R = D | Group 5 | Decrease | Anahata |
| SI | L−R = D | Group 5 | Increase | Anahata |
| UB | L−R = D | Group 5 | Decrease | Svadhishthana |
| HT | (L+R)/2 | Group 6 | Decrease | Anahata |
| SP | (L+R)/2 | Group 6 | Decrease | Manipura |
| LV | L−R = D | Group 6 | Decrease | Manipura |

The meridians which showed a significant functional change along the time lapse and by the influence of the change of room temperature are listed in Table V-28.

*a. Meridians Which Showed Significant Changes*

The meridians of the six groups which showed significant changes due to natural physiological change in meridian function along the time lapse and change in room temperature (high room temperature) in the control-control experiment, are the following: gall bladder, kidney, triple heater, heart constrictor, small intestine, urinary bladder, heart, liver, and spleen. A significant change was recorded in the gall bladder meridian in two of six groups, but only once in the other meridians.

*b. Classification of the Above Meridians According to the Body-Chakra Systems*

The above nine meridians are classified according to the body-Chakra systems : three (aggregate four) meridians belong to the digestive system (Manipura Chakra); four meridians belong to the circulatory system (Anahata Chakra); and two meridians belong to the urogenital system (Svadhishthana Chakra).

*c. Nature of the Change*

The nature of the change is a decrease in the imbalance between the left-right branches in the gall bladder, kidney, heart constrictor, urinary bladder and liver meridians ; a decrease of $(L+R)/2$, that is, a decrease of function and Ki in the heart and spleen meridians; but an increase of imbalance in the left-right branches in the triple heater and small intestine meridians.

Here, an attempt is made to compare the covariance analyses of the control-test data (refer to sections 6. and 7. of D. in the preceeding pages) and the control-control data. In the control-test data analyses, five of the eleven meridians which showed significant changes are the meridians which are closely related to the digestive system (Manipura Chakra). It has been known empirically in the yogic tradition that the Manipura Chakra is the primary receptor of vital force (Prana, Ki, Psi energy, etc.). The result of this experiment indicates that the meridians which are closely related to the Manipura Chakra showed significant changes with higher frequency, and seems to suggest agreement between yogic empirical knowledge and this experimental evidence.

In these control-test data analyses, the significant changes are also found in three meridians which are closely related to the urogenital system (Svadhishthana Chakra); in two meridians which are closely related to the respiratory system (Vishuddhi Chakra) ; and one meridian which is closely related to the circulatory system (Anahata Chakra).

Contrary to these results, in the control-control experiment data analyses in which no mutual influence of Ki took place, the meridians which showed significant changes are the four meridians which are closely related to the digestive system (Manipura Chakra) ; four meridians which are closely related to the circulatory system (Anahata Chakra); and two meridians which belong to the urogenital system (Svadhishthana Chakra). In these control-control data analyses, the meridians which showed significant changes are not only those which are closely related to the Manipura Chakra as in the control-test data analyses.

It can be surmised that from the above that in the control-test experiment, the Ki of subject 2 mainly influenced the meridians closely related to the Manipura Chakra in subject 1.

The nature of the change in all eleven meridians which showed significant changes in the control-test experiment was a decrease of function and Ki and/or a decrease of imbalance in left-right branches. Contrary to this finding, the nature of the change in the control-control experiment was a decrease of function and/or decrease of left-right imbalance in eight of the ten meridians which showed significant changes, and increase of imbalance in the other two meridians. The nature of the change differs between the control-test and control-control experiments ; that is, it might be surmised that the change produced by the mutual influence of Ki is a uniform decrease of function and Ki. This change is contrary to the change as a natural/physiological phenomenon, which is decrease in function and imbalance in some meridians and an increase in others.

### 3. Results of T-Tests and $x^2$ Tests

The fifty subjects for the control-control experiment were divided into five groups, each of which consisted of ten subjects in order of application. Using the same method as described in D.-7., t-tests were performed to examine the frequencies of the significant and insignificant changes between control 1 and control 2 for each meridian. Furthermore, $x^2$ tests were done for the sum of the frequencies of (L+R)/2 and L−R=D, and for each frequency for (L+R)/2 and L−R=D separately.

*a. Group with Application Numbers 1-10*

*i.* In the $x^2$ tests for the sum frequency of (L+R)/2 and L−R=D, $x^2 = 13.03 < x^2_{.05} = 19.68$, which shows no significant difference in the frequency distribution of significant and insignificant changes in individual meridians.

*ii.* $x^2 = 9.23 < x^2_{.05} = 19.68$ for (L+R)/2 shows no significant difference.

*iii.* $x^2 = 14.73 < x^2_{.05} = 19.68$ for L−R=D shows no significant difference.

*b. Group with Application Numbers 11-20*

*i.* $x^2 = 13.54 < x^2_{.05} = 19.68$ for the sum frequency of (L+R)/2 and L−R=D show no significant difference.

*ii.* $x^2 = 9.23 < x^2_{.05} = 19.68$ for (L+R)/2 shows no significant difference.

*iii.* $x^2 = 14.73 < x^2_{.05} = 19.68$ for L−R=D shows no significant difference.

*c. Group wih Application Numbers 21-30*

**Table V − 29**

〔(L+R)/2, | L−R |〕

| | LU | (LI) | HC | TH | HT | SI | (SP) | (LV) | ST | (GB) | (KI) | (UB) |
|---|---|---|---|---|---|---|---|---|---|---|---|---|
| N | 9 | 6 | 14 | 10 | 11 | 10 | 4 | 7 | 9 | 7 | 8 | 3 |
| C | 11 | (14) | 6 | 10 | 9 | 10 | (16) | (13) | 11 | (13) | (12) | (17) |

($\chi 2 = 21.04 > \chi 2$ (r=.05)19.68  df=11)

*i.* $x^2 = 21.04 > x^2_{.05} = 19.68$ for the sum frequency of (L+R)/2 and L−R=D shows a significant difference in the frequency distribution of significant and insignificant changes of the twelve meridians (Table V-29). The meridians which showed a frequency exceeding 11.8, the average frequency of significant change, are the large intestine, spleen, liver, gall bladder, kidney and urinary bladder.

*ii.* $x^2$ tests performed respectively for (L+R)/2 and L−R=D did not show any significant difference.

*iii.* Although no significant difference was found in $x^2$ tests performed respectively for (L+R)/2 and for L−R=D, there was a significant difference in the frequency distribution of significant and insignificant changes among individual meridians in the sum frequencies of (L+R)/2 and L−R=D.

**Table V − 30**

〔(L+R)/2〕 BP

| | LU | LI | HC | TH | HT | SI | SP | LV | ST | GB | KI | UB | Sum |
|---|---|---|---|---|---|---|---|---|---|---|---|---|---|
| N | 4 | 3 | 6 | 5 | 5 | 4 | 2 | 1 | 1 | 1 | 2 | 1 | 35 |
| C | 6 | 7 | 4 | 5 | 5 | 6 | 8 | 9 | 9 | 9 | 8 | 9 | 85 |
| D | 3 | 3 | 1 | 4 | 2 | 4 | 8 | 8 | 9 | 9 | 8 | 9 | 68 |
| I | 3 | 4 | 3 | 1 | 3 | 2 | 0 | 1 | 0 | 0 | 0 | 0 | 17 |

| | LU | LI | HC | TH | HT | SI | SP | LV | ST | GB | KI | UB | Sum |
|---|---|---|---|---|---|---|---|---|---|---|---|---|---|
| | | | — | — | — | | SD | SD | SD | SD | SD | SD | — |
| X | 0.0 | 0.1 | 0.0 | 0.0 | 0.0 | 0.7 | 8.0 | 5.4 | 9.0 | 9.0 | 8.0 | 9.0 | — |
| % | 0.000 | 0.050 | 0.000 | 0.000 | 0.000 | 0.050 | 0.005 | 0.025 | 0.005 | 0.005 | 0.005 | 0.005 | — |
| x | 0.0 | 3.8 | 0.0 | 0.0 | 0.0 | 3.8 | 7.9 | 5.0 | 7.9 | 7.9 | 7.9 | 7.9 | — |

| | LU | LI | HC | TH | HT | SI | SP | LV | ST | GB | KI | UB | Sum |
|---|---|---|---|---|---|---|---|---|---|---|---|---|---|
| D | | | | | | | D | D | D | D | D | D | — |
| I | | | | | | | | | | | | | — |

Table V-30 was made from the results of the $x^2$ test to examine the nature of the change, i.e., whether it was a decrease or an increase in (L+R)/2 of the meridians which showed the higher frequency of significant change than the average in $x^2$ tests table for the sum frequencies of (L+R)/2 and L−R=D. In this table, five of the six meridians (the spleen, liver, gall bladder, kidney, and urinary bladder) showed a significant decrease of function and Ki. As for

L − R = D, no significant difference exists between increase and decrease in the six meridians.

*d. Group with Application Numbers 31-40*

*i.* $x^2 = 16.32 < x^2_{.05} = 19.68$ in $x^2$ tests for the sum frequencies of (L + R)/2 and L − R = D shows no significant difference.

*ii.* $x^2 = 14.70 < x^2_{.05} = 19.68$ in $x^2$ tests for (L + R)/2 shows no significant difference.

*iii.* $x^2 = 11.56 < x^2_{.05} = 19.68$ in $x^2$ tests for L − R = D shows no significant difference.

*e. Group with Application Numbers 41-50*

*i.* $x^2 = 10.98 < x^2_{.05} = 19.68$ in $x^2$ tests for the sum frequencies of (L + R)/2 and L − R = D shows no significant difference.

*ii.* $x^2 = 11.97 < x^2_{.05} = 19.68$ in $x^2$ tests for (L + R)/2 shows no significant difference.

*iii.* $x^2 = 8.40 < x^2_{.05} = 19.68$ in $x^2$ tests for L − R = D shows no significant difference.

***4. Discussion and Consideration of Analyses in Section 3.***

In the analyses of subjects of five groups for the control-control experiment, the significant difference in the frequency distribution of significant and insignificant changes among the twelve individual meridians was solely found in the $x^2$ tests of the sum frequencies of (L + R)/2 and L − R = D of the group with application numbers 21-30. This finding indicates that there is no significant difference in the frequency distributions of the significant changes of meridian function which may have been produced by the time lapse and/or by the influence of change in room temperature and in the insignificant change, in the control-control experiment where the subject was alone in the experiment room. It should be considered that this frequency distribution may have been produced by chance. In the same manner, it could be considered that the significant change produced in each meridian may also have been produced by chance.

On the contrary, in the analyses of the t-tests and $x^2$ tests of the control-test experiment, four of the six groups showed significant differences. This finding seems to indicate that, unlike the control-control experiment, mutual influence of Ki occurred between the two subjects, which resulted in significant changes of the meridian function of subject 1.

## F. Conclusion

### 1. *Results of Covariance Analyses of the Data of the Control-Test Experiment*

#### a. *The Mutual Influence of Ki Can Actually Take Place*

Referring to D.-1.-g., the results of the covariance analyses of the control-test experiment of the six groups (each consisting of ten subjects in order of application) only showed significant changes in two of the twelve meridians. This may be the result of the test arrangement whereby the same pair of subjects acted as subjects 1 and 2 in turn. Due to this arrangment, the subject in the second experiment with the even application number had already been influenced by the Ki of the partner with the odd application number in the first experiment.

Contrary to this finding, a total of eleven (the actual number is seven) of the twelve meridians in six groups showed significant changes in D.-6.-g. : Six groups (each consisting of fifty subjects) were made by six different random tables from sixty subjects. In the analysis arrangement, the fifty subjects were divided into ten groups in which five individuals were equal in ability to receive the influence of Ki. Therefore, the changes produced by the mutual influence of Ki were accurately analyzed.

It can therefore be surmised that the significant changes in meridian function and Ki can be produced by the mutual influence of Ki between numbers of people.

*b. Nature of Change*

The change in these eleven meridians is a decrease of function and Ki and a decrease of the imbalance in the left-right branches of the meridian.

*c. Classification of Seven Meridians Which Showed Significant Changes*

| | |
|---|---|
| The meridians which are closely related to the digestive system (corresponds to the Manipura Chakra) | Stomach, spleen & gall bladder meridians |
| The meridians which are closely related to the urogenital system (corresponds to the Svadhishthana Chakra) | Kidney and urinary bladder meridians |
| The meridians which are closely related to the respiratory system (corresponds to the Vishuddhi Chakra) | Lung meridian |
| The meridians which are closely related to the circulatory system (corresponds to the Anahata Chakra) | Small intestine meridian |

**2. *Meridians Which Showed Significant Changes with High Frequency in the Analyses of T-Tests and $x^2$ Tests of the Control-Test Experiment***

Referring to the discussion and considerations in D.-8., the changes produced by the mutual influence of Ki between subjects was examined by the t-tests and $x^2$ tests which were explained in D.-7. The meridians which showed significant changes with high frequency in the six groups (each consisting of ten subjects in order of application) are the lung, gall bladder, liver, spleen, kidney and urinary bladder.

They may be classified as follows :

| | |
|---|---|
| The meridians which are closely related to the digestive system (corresponds to the Manipura Chakra) | Gall bladder, spleen & liver meridians |
| The meridians which are closely related to the urogenital system (corresponds to the Svadhishthana Chakra) | Kidney and urinary bladder meridians |
| The meridians which are closely related to the respiratory system (corresponds to the Vishuddhi Chakra) | Lung meridian |

The above classification closely corresponds to the classification made in F.-1.-c.

### 3. *Meridians Which Are Most Easily Affected by the Mutual Influence of Ki*

#### a. *Meridians Which Are Most Easily Influenced*

| | |
|---|---|
| The meridians which are closely related to the digestive system | Spleen & gall bladder meridians |
| The meridians which are closely related to the urogenital system | Kidney & urinary bladder meridians |
| The meridians which are closely related to the respiratory system | Lung meridian |

The above five meridians can be considered the meridians most easily affected by the mutual influence of Ki between people as they displayed high significant changes in both the different analyses. As for the classification according to the body-Chakra system, the meridians which are closely related to the digestive, urogenital and respiratory systems are easily influenced. The meridians which are closely related to the circulatory system only once showed a significant change.

*b. Nature of Change*

Referring to D.-8., the change observed in the meridians displaying significant changes is in each case decrease of function and Ki. This finding coincides with the analyses in D.-6.-g.

Therefore it can be concluded that the change of the meridians which showed significant change by the mutual influence of Ki is either a decrease of function and Ki, or a decrease of the imbalance between the left and right branches.

### *4. Which of the Normal or Abnormal Meridians Are Most Easily Affected?*

D.-2.,3.,4. examines whether the meridians displaying significant changes by the mutual influence of Ki more often coincided with the meridians with normal function, or those with abnormal function. These analyses showed that a normal or abnormal condition is not closely connected to the changes produced by the mutual influence of Ki.

### *5. Authentication of the Results of the Control-Test Experiment with the Control-Control Experiment*

The procedure in E. was conducted in order to authenticate the results of the control-test experiment. Covariance analyses, t-tests, and $x^2$ tests were performed between the data of control 1 and control 2. The results obtained are explained in E.-2.,4.

*a. Comparison of Covariance Analyses Results*

*i. Meridians Which Showed Significant Changes*

When the covariance analyses of the control-test data (refer to D.-6.,7.) were compared with those of the control-control data, five of the eleven meridians which showed significant changes in the control-test experiment are the meridians closely related to the Manipura Chakra. This

Chakra, according to yogic tradition, is the main receptor of Prana (Ki, Psi energy). The test results showing that the meridians which are closely related to this Chakra most frequently showed changes seem to correspond to this traditional empirical knowledge.

In the control-control experiment, however, which was arranged so that no influence of Ki could take place between the subjects, significant changes were not only shown in meridians closely related to the Manipura Chakra.

From the above, it can be surmised that the influence of Ki between people occurs mainly in the Manipura Chakra and its connected meridians.

*ii. Nature of Change*

The change observed in all eleven meridians which showed significant changes in the control-test experiment was decrease of meridian function and Ki or decrease of the imbalance between the left-right branches. The change observed in eight of ten meridians which showed significant changes in the control-control experiment was a decrease of meridian function and Ki or a decrease of the imbalance between the left-right branches, but the other two meridians showed a significant increase in the left-right imbalance. Here, the results of the control-control experiment differ from those of the control-test experiment. It might be possible to surmise that the meridian function and imbalance decreases and also increases as a natural and physiological phenomenon, but that it uniformly decreases by the mutual influence of Ki.

*b. Comparison of T-Tests and $x^2$ Test Results*

While one of the five groups showed a significant change in the t-test and $x^2$ tests analyses of the control-control experiment data, four of the six groups showed significant changes in those of the control-test experiment data. It can be considered that this is indicative of the mutual influence of Ki actually having taken place between the two subjects in the control-test experiment, and that this produced significant changes in subject 1's meridian function.

To conclude Part Ⅰ, in the next chapter the author will explain the essential difference between Ki nd Psi energy.

Notes for Chapter V

1) *Internal Ki*: If you are interested in the electrophysiological studies of 'internal Ki', please refer to " Meridians and Ki ", *Research for Religion and Parapsychoplogy*, (No.16), December 1986 ; and *Ki no Nagare no Sokutei, Shindan, to Chiryo*, (Measurment, Diagnosis, and Treatment of Ki), Shukyo Shinri Shuppan, 1985, by the author. (under translation into English) (tr.)

2) *Sei Points*: Near the tips of the fingers and toes are the Sei (Jing in Chinese and Well in English) points, where the meridians either begin or end, depending on the direction of the flow. These Sei points have traditionally been known to sensitively reflect the condition of the meridians to which they belong. Refer to note 2) of Chapter Ⅱ for AMI measurements. (tr.)

3) Refer to note 6) of Chapter Ⅲ. (tr.)

4) *These are four classifications of abnormality of meridian function monitored with the AMI*:

* Deficiency indicates a deficient state of Ki and a lowered function of the meridian.
* Excessive indicates an excessive state of Ki and an excited function of the meridian.
* Imbalance indicates a left-right difference between bilateral branches of the meridian.
* Inversion indicates the inversion of functional competition between the traditional Yin-Yang pairs of the meridian. (tr.)

5) *Group with application numbers 31-41*: After the test, the data of subject 32 was distorted on the computer disk and analyses became impossible. Therefore this number must be omitted in this paper, resulting in non-regularity of numbers.

# VI. CORRELATION BETWEEN KI, MERIDIANS AND PSI-ENERGY (ABILITY)

Through my long-term yoga practices, spiritual consultations and psychic healing, scientific study of paranormal phenomena, and biophysical studies of Ki and meridians, it has become clear empirically and clinically that the Psi energy which plays an important role in spiritual consultations and psychic healing is closely connected to the Chakras of yoga and meridians and Ki of Chinese medicine.

To accumulate evidence for this hypothesis, more experiments (such as those described in the previous chapters of this book) have been conducted in the past five to six years.

### 1. *Elucidation of the Light Experiment*

*a.* Light generation was frequently monitored in the vicinity of the Svadhishthana and Anahata Chakras, especially in front of the former. This, together with the other values monitored by the Chakra Instrument, suggests activation of the Svadhishthana Chakra in M.Y. Furthermore, it can be surmised that Psi energy was converted into physical energy (light) through this activated Svadhishthana Chakra — a type of psychokinesis.

*b.* In the AMI data of M.Y., abnormal function was monitored in the kidney, urinary bladder and small intestine meridians, which are empirically and clinically known to be closely connected to the urogenital system and the Svadhishthana Chakra. This evidence verifies the close connection between the Svadhishthna Chakra and these meridians.

*c.* From *a.* and *b.*, it can be surmised that the Svadhishthana Chakra actually exists.

### 2. *Elucidation of ESP Tests and Meridian Measurements*

*a.* As opposed to the chance-scorer class (who did not exhibit the presence of ESP ability), the Psi-hit class (who exhibited the presence of ESP ability) and Psi-miss class (who could not sufficiently exhibit this ability) showed significant difference between the control data and ESP test data in Ki and function of the spleen, stomach and liver meridians, which are closely connected to the Manipura Chakra ; and in the kidney, urinary bladder and small intestine meridians, which are closely connected to the Svadhishthana Chakra. Both the Manipura and Svadhishthana Chakras are known for ESP ability.

This is objective evidence that ESP ability, a type of Psi ability, belongs to the Manipura and Svadhishthana Chakras.

*b.* This evidence also suggests that the Manipura Chakra and its ESP ability are closely related to the spleen, stomach, and liver meridians, and that the Svadhishthana Chakra and its ESP ability are closely connected to the kidney, urinary bladder and small intestine meridians.

*c.* Furthermore, this evidence validates the existence of the Manipura and Svadhishthana Chakras.

### 3. *Elucidation of the PK Test and Meridian Measurements*

*a.* When the sender emitted Psi energy from the Ajna Chakra, an increase of Ki and function in the urinary bladder meridian, which is closely connected to the Ajna Chakra, was monitored. The results indicated a close connection between the urinary bladder meridian, and the Ajna Chakra and its PK energy.

*b.* When Psi energy was injected into the Chukyoku (CV3) and Kangen (CV4) points of the recipient, an increase of Ki and function was monitored in the liver meridian which courses in these points and is closely connected to the urogenital system. This data indicates that PK phenomena were actually generated by Psi energy from the Ajna Chakra.

*c.* This evidence, although indirect, verifies that Psi energy was actually emitted from the Ajna Chakra of the sender, that the Psi energy was actually injected in the directed area of the recipient, and that this increased the meridian function and Ki of the recipient meridian which courses in the directed area.

*d.* From *a.*, *b.* and *c.*, it can be concluded that the Ajna Chakra actually exists.

### 4. *Elucidation of the Experiments of Mutual Influence of Ki*

The following can be concluded on the basis of the covariance analyses, t-tests and $\chi^2$ tests of the control-control experiments and control-test experiment data.

*a.* One subject mutually influences the other subject's meridian function simply by their being together in the same room.

*b.* The meridians which are susceptible to this influence and the corresponding body-Chakra systems are as follows : the spleen and gall bladder meridians (digestive system — Manipura Chakra) ; kidney and urinary bladder meridians (urogenital system — Svadhishthana Chakra); lung meridian (respiratory system — Vishuddhi Chakra). The heart and heart constrictor meridians (circulatory system — Anahata Chakra) were not significantly influenced.

*c.* Among the meridians which were significantly influenced, the frequency of significant change was highest in the meridians which correspond to the Manipura Chakra. This data suggests that the mutual influence of Ki between people takes place in the highest degree in the meridians which correspond to the digestive system and Manipura Chakra.

*d.* The nature of the above significant change is the decrease of function and Ki and decrease of the imbalance in the left-right branches.

*e.* Whether the function of the meridians is normal or abnormal is not closely connected with susceptibility to the mutual influence of Ki.

5. ***Conclusions of 1.– 4.***

*a.* The awakening and activation of the Chakras was monitored with the Chakra Instrument and recorded in the chart as changes in the bio-energy field. The existence of the Chakras, Psi ability and Psi phenomena caused by this ability was objectively and scientifically, although indirectly, evidenced.

*b.* There is a close connection between the Svadhishthana Chakra and the kidney, urinary bladder and small intestine meridians.

*c.* Psychokinetic ability also emerges through the function of the Svadhishthana Chakra.

*d.* ESP ability emerges through a function of the Manipura and Svadhishthana Chakras.

*e.* The Manipura Chakra and its ESP ability is closely related to the spleen, stomach and liver meridians.

*f.* The Svadhishthana Chakra and its ESP ability are closely related to the kidney, urinary bladder and small intestine meridians.

*g.* PK ability is also derived from the Ajna Chakra.

*h.* The Ajna Chakra and its PK ability are closely related to the urinary bladder meridian.

*i.* Psi energy was actually emitted from the Ajna Chakra and generated changes in the meridian which courses in its directed area.

*j.* A mutual influence of Ki between people who are in the same room but have no physical contact actually occurs. This influence takes place most easily in the spleen and gall bladder meridians, which are closely connected to the Manipura Chakra.

### 6. *The Difference between Psi Energy and Ki*

#### *a. Psi Energy Is Beyond the Restrictions of Physical Time and Space*

In the ESP test, the cards were placed face-down on the table. The sense of sight using light energy was therefore not involved in reading the face of the cards. ESP ability is essentially different from abilities which function under the restrictions of time and space in the physical dimension (such as the senses) and is also different from functions of physical energy (such as light). Of course, when the content perceived by means of ESP is brought to the consciousness, it follows the physical and physiological processes of the brain and is then limited by physical time and space.

When I perform psychic healing using PK ability from the Ajna Chakra, I 'feel' difficulty in sending energy into the other person, even if that person is next to me, if they doubt me or are close-minded. On the other hand, if the person trusts me and has an open mind, it would be very easy to send PK energy, even if the person were overseas. The successful function of Psi energy is not restricted by physical time and space.

For example, in one case, a child who lived far from Tokyo was hospitalized after having suffered from a high fever for over a week, and in another, a woman, also far from Tokyo, was in serious condition due to excessive bleeding during an operation. After being contacted by their families, I prayed and sent Psi energy to them, and they were miraculously restored to health. It has been my experience that the successful transmission of Psi energy depends not on time and space, but on the openness of one's mind.

While the light experiment was being conducted with the Chakra Instrument, two experimenters noticed that the clock (without batteries) on the wall outside the shielded room started and stopped several times before and after the light generation. The energy which started the clock running was not the energy of the physical dimension ; if it were, it could not have penetrated the thick wall of the shielded room.

Psi energy seems to be a non-physical energy which is beyond the restrictions of time and space. On the other hand, Ki seems to be an energy which falls under these restrictions.

*b. Is Ki under the Restriction of Physical Time and Space?*

As was seen, the mutual influence of Ki took place between subjects 1 and 2 while they were sitting about one meter apart in the same room. The meridians which showed significant change are summarized in section *4.* of this chapter. While the control-control experiment with subject 1 was being performed, subject 2 remained in a separate room, five to six meters from the experiment room. The nature of the change in this experiment differs from the control-test experiment where a mutual exchange of Ki between subjects seems to have taken place.

The mutual exchange of Ki did not take place when subject 2 was in a separate room from subject 1. I therefore think that it can be concluded that Ki is under the restriction of physical time and space.

We might think, however, that some tension or hypnotic effect could have occurred between the subjects when subject 2 was sitting in proximity to subject 1. If there were some tension, then a functional change should have been produced in the heart and heart constrictor meridians, as was observed in Chapter Ⅲ. These are not, however, the meridians which were significantly influenced by the mutual influence of Ki in the control-test experiment. As for the possibility of hypnotic effect, both subjects 1 and 2 were fully awake at the time of the experiment, and it is not possible to consider that they were in a state subject to suggestion and hypnosis.

### 7. *Overall Conclusions of Part I*

As a conclusion to Part I, the following can be said :

The Chakras, Psi ability, Psi energy, meridians and Ki actually exist, and there is a close connection among them. It is true, however, that the mechanism of their inter-related function is barely known at present.

Psi energy is beyond the limitations of physical time and space, while Ki energy is not. The reciprocal function between these two energies is not yet known.

PART II

# TOWARDS THE UNIFICATION OF SCIENCE AND RELIGION

## A. The World of Science

### *1. Science*

Science deals with natural objects perceived by the senses either directly or through scientific instrumentation. A linear chain of cause and effect is conjectured in the process of the generation, continuance and extinction of the object, and a hypothesis is then established. If the generation, continuation and extinction of the object is reproduced in a series of experiments being conducted on the basis of that hypothesis, the hypothesis is accepted as a scientific truth or theory.

### *2. **The Object in Modern Science** -The way the object of modern science is seen depends on the means of observation-*

Werner Heisenberg says that the nature observed by scientists is not nature itself, but instead it is nature appearing to the observer in accordance with the investigation methods.

Fritjof Capra says that his intention to use a certain observation method with a certain experimental arrangement somehow determines the characteristics of the electrons observed in the experiment ; and that the electrons, therefore, may not be objective and independent from either the observation method or the observer's mind.

In the mechanistic world view of Isaac Newton and Rene Descartes, mind and matter are separate entitites. In their view, the material world is a huge machine consisting of complex aggregates of matter — it is a world which exists and functions on its own mechanisms completely independent from the mind.

Heisenberg and Capra have observed, however, that in the world of subatomic particles and quantum theory, matter shows different characteristics in accordance with the type of observation and investigation method. In other words, the more precise scientific tools and instrumentation become, the more limited the aspect of matter that science can "see" in a single observation. For example, subatoms exhibit particle properties or wave properties depending on the method of observation. Capra says that subatomic particles are not isolated separate entitites, but must be understood in terms of interactions with the experiment and subsequent act of observation. He further says that the observation (observer) in atomic physics is not independent from, but is involved in the world of the object.

In classical Newtonian physics, which deals with natural phenomena in their macroscopic aspects within a Cartesian mechanistic view of nature, the material world exists independent of human observers. However, in the theory of subatomic particles, the observation (observer) and natural objects interact with each other and the nature which is grasped in terms of such interactions is treated as the object of natural science.

Is it true that natural science explores all the objects of investigation by means of methods based upon mutual interactions? The answer is no; instead, natural science uses approximation.

### *3. Approximation*

Physicists conduct investigations on selected groups of objects among various natural phenomena, and neglect those which seem comparatively unrelated to these groups. They try to understand and explain multitudes of other phenomena with the theories and laws obtained from the phenomena of the selected groups. This method is called approximation, and so the theory and model of natural science is only an approximate representation of the real events in nature. Therefore it is impossible to simultaneously comprehend all aspects of events in the research of natural science.

This inability is the limitation of research in natural science. In spite of this limitation, however, modern physics seems to be approaching the more essential domains of material nature.

### *4. There is No Solid Material "Stuff" on the Level of Atoms*

According to classical physics, it is thought that all substances are made of ultimate constituents and all phenomena in nature can be explained by the fundamental laws which concern these ultimate concepts. These concepts were, in turn, considered to be solid and unchangeable. As research of particle physics progressed, however, physicists discovered that the subatomic particles are not composed of ultimate constituents, but are more reasonably regarded to be "condensation of energy" or "energy packed in form". This energy is related to the activity and the process through which particles are recognized.

It is said that subatomic particles are not particles as static three-dimensional matter, but four-dimensional entities within the continuum of space-time. The subatomic particles manifest themselves both as matter with mass in the aspect of space, and as various processes which inherently involve the energy equivalent to its mass in the aspect of time. Therefore, there is no three-dimensional, static and solid matter on the level of subatoms.

According to Einstein's formula $E = mc^2$ ($m$ = mass, $c$ = velocity of light), mass is a form of energy and not a static solid substance. In research on subatomic particles, it is well-known that the $\gamma$-ray, which is the short electromagnetic wave originating from radioactive elements, vanishes by creating an electron and a positron (a positron has the same mass as the electron but has a positive charge). The $\gamma$-ray (energy) is thus transformed into matter. For this transformation to take place, the energy of the $\gamma$-ray in the quantity of $(m \times c^2)$ is necessary to generate the pair of particles.

When these positrons enter into the matter and encounter electrons, they disappear and generate the $\gamma$-ray of energy equivalent to their mass. That is, the positron and the electron are extinguished. Mass, then, is not permanent but is a form of energy.

However, a question still remains. Namely, what is it that generates electrons and positrons by "packing" the energy of the $\gamma$-ray when the $\gamma$-ray creates them, although admittedly there is no solid matter on the level of subatoms? Furthermore, what is it that makes this energy return to its original $\gamma$-ray form? Is this the subatom itself, or as an entity in the four-dimensional continuum of space-time, which becomes matter in space and energy processes in time, as Capra suggests? This question will be discussed in the section on experiments conducted at the Institute for Religious Psychology.

Some ontological thoughts on the view of matter in modern physics, particularly the interaction between the observation and object of observation will be given below.

### 5. *Science Stands on the Confrontation (Dichotomy) of Subject and Object*

In Newton's classical physics and the Cartesian dualistic theory, the material world exists independently from the mind and functions on its own mechanisms. Here the mind is a simple observer of a natural phenomon of matter. Thus, mind and matter are independent and separate.

As scientific technology advanced and it became possible to observe matter on a subatomic level, however, it was discovered that the act of observation itself influences the material phenomenon as an object of observation. As Capra and Heisenberg say, the characteristics of the matter to be observed change depending on the observation methods. An interaction takes place between the act of observation and the object of observation, i.e., material phenomenon. This was not believed to be true according to classical physics. Capra says, "Because it is the mind that determines the method of observation, the mind which observes is not independent and unrelated from the phenomenon as an object, but is involved in it."

After careful consideration, however, it is evident that the observer's mind is not directly involved in and exerting an influence on the object, but that the particular configuration of the physical instrumentation at the observation influences the interactive processes of the object. What the observer's mind does is to determine the instrumentation to be used at the observation. That is, the kind of instrumentation and the way it will be used (which is determined by the mind) influences the material phenomenon as object. The mind, therefore, does not directly influence the material phenomenon, but it stands as the observer outside the object. The separation (confrontation) remains between the observer (mind, subject) and the material phenomenon (matter, object).

Contrary to this separation, in the world of religion, mind and matter (or subject and object) are unified, and the mind directly influences matter. Furthermore, the mind can create or annihilate physical energy or matter which has mass. Here is the fundamental difference between science and religion.

## B. The World of Religion

Religion is a way of living in relation to the Greater Being, God, or the Absolute.

### *1. Faith*

Faith is the way of living everyday life with devotion to God or the Absolute, and observing the morals and regulations given by Him. This assumption is fundamental in the religions founded by the Semitic peoples — Christianity, Judaism, and Islam. In these religions, there is an insurmountable separation between God as the Creator, and humans and nature as the created. It is impossible for the created human to attain oneness with God. What human beings can do is to live in relation to God and obey His commandments with devotion and faith.

## 2. *Ascetic Life Toward God or the Absolute*

The religions of the Orient — Hinduism and Buddhism, for example — teach both the possiblity for humans to evolve to higher dimensions of being and toward oneness with God, and the practices necessary for this evolution. One of them is Chosaku (transcendent action : action where one applies oneself to the appointed task without desiring any result from the action, and where one becomes the action itself, casting off the consciousness of 'I am doing'). If one can do such actions even once or twice a day, one can, in every action, discard the one who does the action and desires the result, and prepare oneself to progress to a higher dimension which transcends one's present mode of being. When this preparation is made and the negation of the present mode of living proceeds to its culmination, there is an inflow of power, negation of the present mode of being, and support for the transition into the higher dimension, given by God or the Absolute. One can then spiritually leap into the higher dimensions and can attain Satori or enlightenment.

Another practice which enables one to attain Satori (or enlightenment) is concentration and meditation. One can be one with the object through concentrating and meditating on it, and can realize the world of oneness where the meditating mind (subject) and what is meditated on (object) are unified. This world of oneness can neither be described as mind nor matter, but can be both mind and matter, and is a world which embraces both. This world can be called the world of Topos (place)[1].

In the state of concentration, the concentrating mind and the object of concentration (e.g. Mandalas, holy statues, Chakras) are still confronting one another. Through concentration on an object, mental function is simplified. Through deeper concentration on the object, this simplified mind gradually breaks through the shell of existence which one has in the present dimension of being. Here one reaches the state of meditation. When this breakthrough of one's present mode of being partially occurs, there is a partial union with the object. When it wholly occurs, and a total unification with the object is made possible by the inflow of power from the Higher Entity, a leap into the higher dimension or the world of Topos is possible. Here is a world of total union of subject and object. In this state of being, one has become a god or being as Topos[2], although the form remains human.

Is such a transition simply a subjective occurrence? Is it mere imagination? The answer is no. It is an objective reality in the world of Topos or a world of gods. It is not mere subjective imagination but it is that which actually underlies, controls, supports and vitalizes the realities of the world experienced by humans.

### 3. Characteristics of the Being as Topos

When one attains this state, one will be endowed with the following abilities and attributes:

#### a. *All Is in Oneself*

The consciousneness that all is in 'myself' and that 'I' am the World of Universe, wells up within one who has attained this state. Furthermore, if one concentrates the mind (superconsciousness, universal consciousness) on one particular existence, one can intuitively grasp the whole picture of its existence throughout the process of the past, present, future at the same time in many dimensions. Furthermore one can enter into the matter (object) and observe it as the matter itself.

#### b. *Prajna (Wisdom of the Other Shore)*

All is in oneself and it is possible to know the essence of all in the many dimensions of being. For example, wholly and intuitively overviewing the events, the way of being, and nature of a soul in this and other worlds in the past and present, it naturally comes to mind what is necessary for the soul. What should be done for the earth and for humanity are also naturally known. Indeed, what is now most important for the earth and humanity is the evolution of consciousness and spiritual growth.

c. *Love*

The wisdom which intuits the multi-dimensional existence of all at the same time manifests itself in the action which gives life to and supports all that is in oneself — the self as the being as Topos — and which enables their spiritual growth and evolution. One's love is not limited to the Love for human beings, but embraces all, including nature, the earth, and spiritual entitities.

d. *Freedom*

Although one is the being as Topos standing on the union of subject and object, one exists as a human until one's physical karma in this physical dimension is worked out. However, in its essential nature, one is beyond the human mind and physical body, and is free from their function as well as the instinct for self-preservation. The being as Topos, who is liberated from the world of personal karma which is governed by the principle of self-preservation (the principle of matter), is free from self-existence as an individual. The higher the dimension of the world of Topos, the less individual existence there is, and thus the more perfect freedom is obtained, because spiritual evolution is achieved through self-negation.

e. *Consciousness as Topos (Superconsciousness) Can Directly Control Matter*

The ordinary human mind does not have a direct influence on matter. However, the consciousness (superconsciousness) of one as Topos can generate light in a light-proof shielded room, or extinguish or create matter without any physical means. Or it can heal the sick and enable the dying to survive. It can control the weather and can have an influence on the world of spirits. Such control of natural phenomena in the physical world provides evidence that spiritual evolution into higher beings in the world of Topos through self-negation by way of transcendent action and meditation is not merely the production of imagination.

## C. Experiments for the Elucidation of Psi Energy

We scientifically investigated people who, to a certain degree, had attained a unification with their guardian spirit and who had control over matter through religious practices coupled with their innate paranormal ability. In one of the experiments with subject M.Y.[3], light was generated in a light-proof shielded room. By explaining the experiment, I will give evidence of mental control over matter by one whose consciousness has achieved a certain degree of spiritual evolution.

### *1. A Light Experiment and Its Data*

*a. Experiment Room*

The experiment room constructed on the third floor of the Institute for Religious Psychology consists of a shielded room and a measurement room in which various equipment is installed (Figure 1). The shielded room is about 160 cm × 220 cm in size, and the surface is completely covered with copper plates (thickness : 0.4 mm). The inside of the walls are lined with lead plates (thickness : 5 mm) and the outer walls are of concrete (thickness : 15 cm). The space inside the room is thus shielded from various forms of electromagnetic waves.

*b. Purpose of the Experiment*

Whether the Psi energy (mental energy) of a psychic subject (M.Y., female) and her male friend (also psychic)[4] created any change in the electric and magnetic fields and/or generated light in the shielded room was to be investigated.

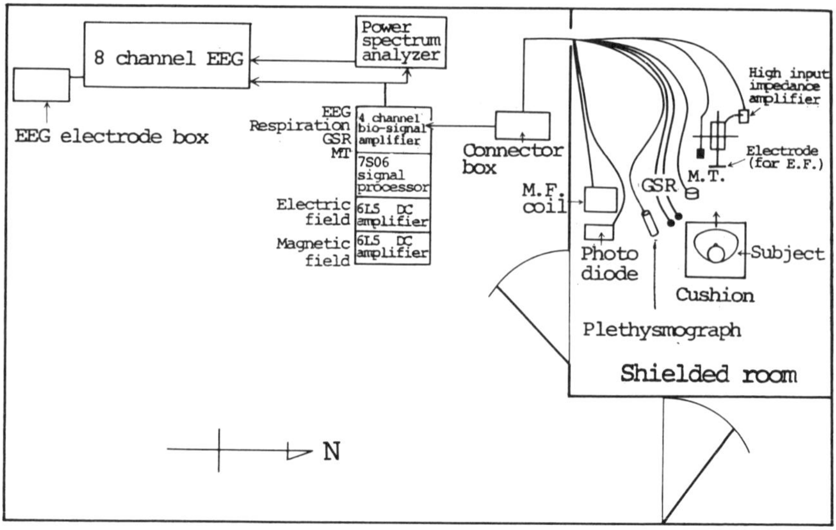


**Figure 1**: Experimental Set-up

*c. Experimental Procedure*

The subject sat on a cushion (Figure 2) in a yoga half-lotus position (siddhasana) with minimal clothing in order to prevent the generation of static electricity from the clothing. The electrodes to monitor respiration, GSR (Galvanic Skin Response), plethysmograph, and minor tremor (micro-vibration of the skin) were attached to her wrists, finger tips, nose, etc. In the shielded room, the sensor to detect the potential change in the electric field and a photoelectric cell sensitive to a wide diapason of light frequencies were installed 30 cm in front of the subject; the MF coil (which detects changes in the magnetic field) was installed 50 cm in front and to the left of the subject; and the video camera (VHS) to record light generation 1.2m to the left of the subject. The subject's male friend, who was 25 years old and practicing Aikido at the time, sat in siddhasana in a corner outside the shielded room and sent psychic power to M.Y.

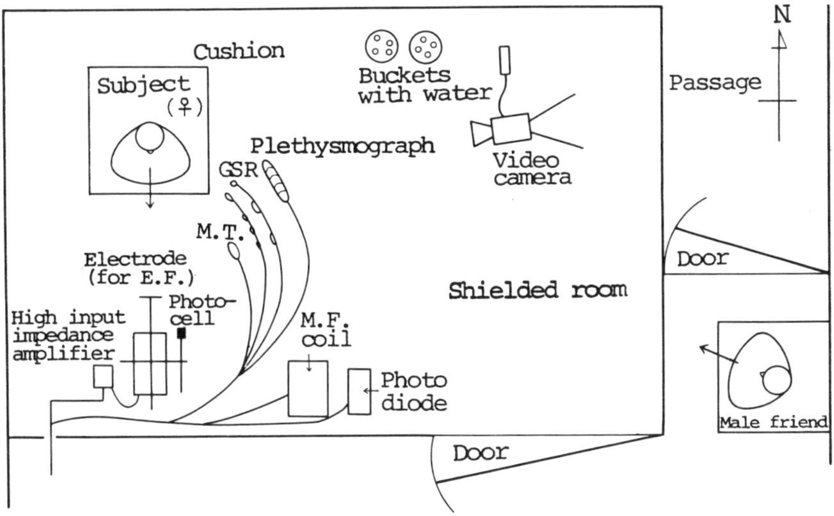


**Figure 2**: Experimental Set-up in the Shielded Room

The experiment, which was observed throughout, was arranged so that these subjects were unable to have any sensory communication. The subject was first monitored in a relaxed state before the concentration period. Next, the subject and her friend entered meditation, the former concentrating on the Ajna Chakra and strongly wishing for light to be generated in the room. M.Y. was monitored continuously throughout the session. After this session, the male friend stopped his meditation, and M.Y. alone continued the meditation and was monitored. After the experiment, M.Y. reported what she had felt during the experiment. When she perceived and received the Psi energy from her friend, and when she received power from and felt a oneness with her guardian spirit, a "universal power" (her own words), she felt a flash of light several times. As she closed her eyes while meditating during the experiment, she felt light generation as something brightening her surroundings.

*d. Data Analyses*

*i. Video Recording*

Pictures taken from the video camera recorded the generation of light in the shielded room.

**Figure 3**: Drawing of M.Y. in the Shielded Room

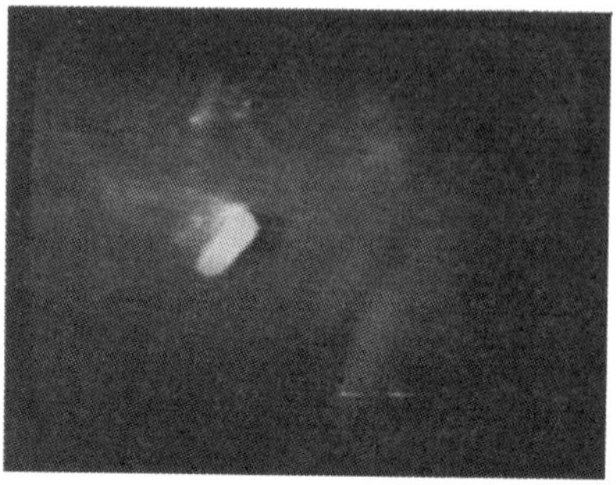

**Picture 1**: M.Y. in the Shielded Room and Torch Light

**Picture 2**: Light Generated through Psi-energy (Large)

**Picture 3**: Light Generated through Psi-energy (Small)

In Picture 1, the left and upper half of M.Y.'s body, and the flashlight which was shone in the room for comparison are shown, although the photograph is not clear. (Refer to the drawing of the location of M.Y. in the shielded room in Figure 3.)

The size of the light is comparatively large (diameter: about 1 cm) in Picture 2 and it has a comparatively small diameter (about 5mm) in Picture 3, showing a decrease in

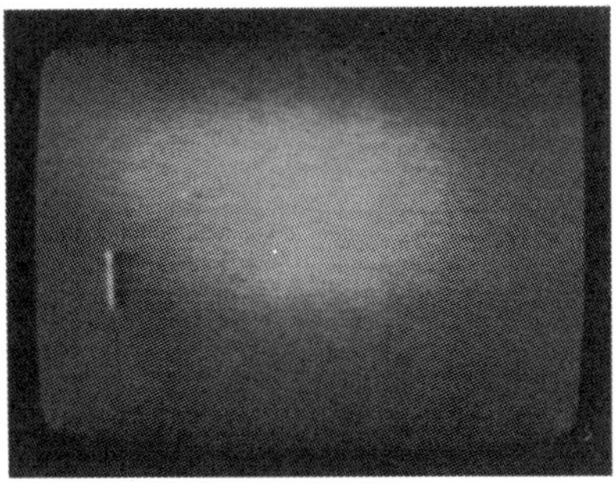

**Picture 4**: Light Generated through Psi-energy (Two)

size. In Picture 4, the light was filmed emerging from M. Y.'s lower abdomen and rising to the chest area.

In the video recording, the light was not always unified and was not continuously bright to the end. Sometimes it split into two or three parts (Picture 4). It moved up and down, right and left, and sometimes emerged for a second and disappeared. Sometimes it remained constant for a few seconds in front of her chest or between her eyebrows, then became brighter and dimmer. However, in every case, the light emerged in the area of her lower abdomen (which corresponds to the Svadhishthana Chakra of Yoga tradition). The color changed alternately from red to purple.

*ii. Polygraph*

*Before Concentration*

Figure 4 is the polygraph taken during the relaxation before any attempt at concentration. The fourth recording from the top is the photoelectric cell, which is sensitive to a wide diapason of light frequencies. At the beginning of the measurements, a rounded mountain-like wave was recorded when the flashlight was shone in the shielded room. Another round wave was recorded when the door was opened and light entered the room. The top recording of this figure is the recording of the magnetic field, and only the natural fluctuation of the

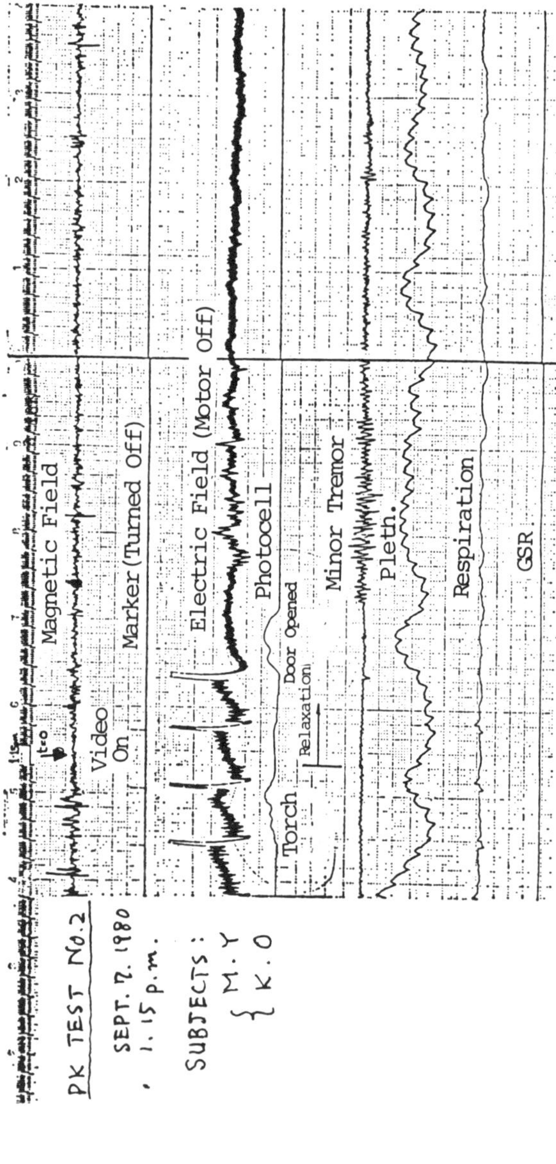


**Figure 4**: Polygraph — Torch light and when the door was opened

earth magnetism was monitored. The third is the recording of the electric field and monitors static potential changes in the electric field around the subject. Large spike-like fluctuations were recorded when the sensing electrode was moved back and forth by motor, but the line was flat when this electrode movement was stopped.

The fifth is the minor tremor (MT), which monitors the micro-vibration of the subject's skin, and indicates that M.Y. moved her body slightly after the door was opened. The sixth is the plethysmograph and the base line fluctuation of this recording indicates either that the subject was excited, or that she moved her hands slightly. The seventh is the respiration recording. Although the amplification was insufficient, the rate is readable. The bottom reflects GSR. It may be due to low amplification that this recording appears flat.

*During Concentration*

Concentration began at the point indicated by the arrow in Figure 5. After beginning the concentration, only the natural fluctuation of the earth magnetism was recorded in the magnetic field. No change was monitored in the electric field. Minor tremor and respiration rates were stable, and the base line of the plethysmograph showed more regularity.

After several minutes, lights were generated and recorded in the polygraph (Figure 5). While the light generation was detected in the photoelectric cell, there was no change other than the natural fluctuation of the earth magnetism in the magnetic field. No clear correlation between the light detection by the photoelectric cell and magnetic field fluctuation was recorded in this data, although more might have been discovered if the signal had been taken with greater amplification and faster chart speed. There was no change in the electric field. As is indicated in Figure 5, the recording of the photoelectric cell was divided into segments (B), (C), (D), and

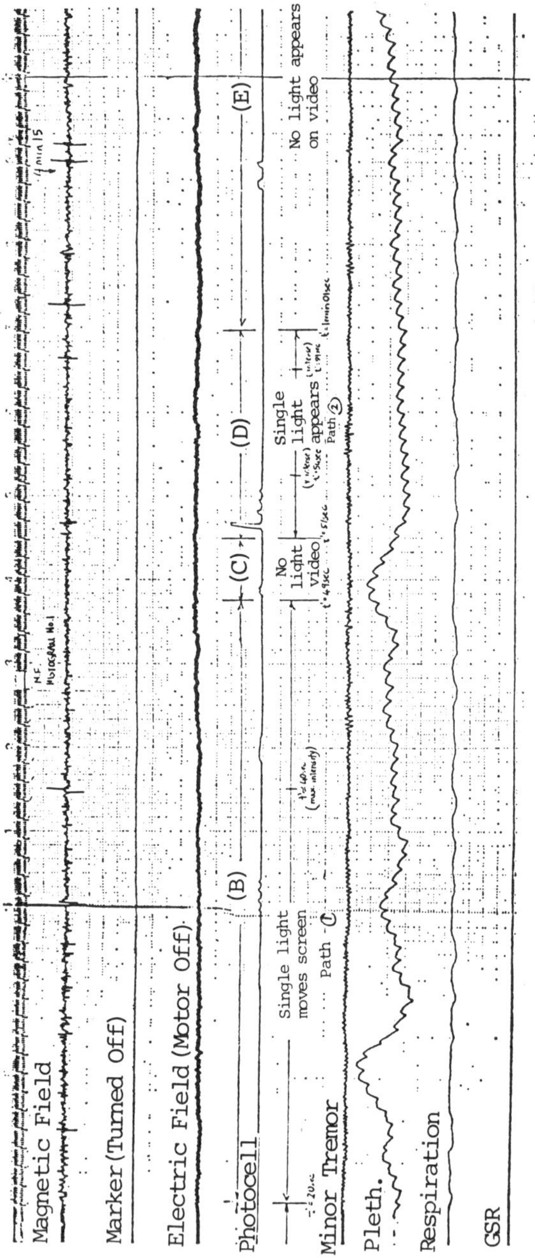


**Figure 5**: Polygraph — During concentration and meditation

(E). In each segment rectangular or spike-like light signals were recorded.

Three low-amplitude light signals and a signal of low amplitude but of large wave-length were recorded in segment (B) ; a low amplitude wave was recorded in segment (C) ; a high amplitude spike-like wave was recorded at the beginning of segment (D), followed by three low-amplitude waves ; and two low amplitude waves were recorded in segment (E). The amplitude of the light signals indicates the intensity of the light; bright light is indicated by the high-amplitude signal and less bright by the low amplitude signal. The short wave length signal indicates a momentary recording of light. The long wave length signals indicate a continuous recording of light for one to two seconds. The time-related comparative analysis between the video recording and polygraph reveals that the light in segments (C) and (E) were not recorded on the video film.

As regards the electrophysiological recordings in these segments, the base line fluctuation of the plethysmograph decreased, no GSR signals were recorded, and the respiration was shallow. These recordings indicate that the subject was relaxed throughout these segments. However, it should be pointed out that the sensitivity of the instruments used in these particular electrophysiological measurements was not sufficient for any definite conclusions to be drawn.

### 2. Considerations

#### a. *Unification of the Subject and Object, and Psi Energy*

According to subject M.Y., the time when light was generated in the pitch-dark shielded room corresponded to the moment when she felt the reception of Psi energy from her male friend, or when she felt the inflow of power from and oneness with a "universal power". The Psi energy sent from her male friend was not physical energy in the form of electromagnetic waves or other vibrations, because the inside of the room is completely shielded from such. It can then be surmised that the perceived energy might have been magnetic lines or radioactive rays, both of which can pass through the walls of the shielded room. However, it has been confirmed through parapsychological experiments on PK (Psychokinesis) and ESP (Extrasensory Perception) conducted at this Institute and elsewhere, that the Psi energy which is thought to play an important role in the occurrence of PK and ESP phenomena is not restricted by physical time and space. It would not be wrong to consider that the Psi energy perceived by M.Y. was not physical energy. It could be concluded that this energy is the energy of the mind, energy which is not restricted by time and space.

Unification with the "universal power" is the oneness of subject and object which supports both mind and matter, transcending the interaction between them as was described in the section on "the world of religion". The Pure Spirit[5] which functions in this world of oneness is not the ordinary consciousness (mind) which functions under the control of physical forces, dependent upon the physical body and in confrontation with matter. As was explained, the Pure Spirit is both independent of matter and, at the same time, supports matter. Psi energy can be surmised to be a mental energy which belongs to the Pure Spirit in a higher dimension of being. So it is beyond the restrictions of matter in time and space. The physical walls of the shielded room are no obstacle in such a world of being. It is impossible to directly verify this existence scientifically, because scientific instrumentation can only monitor material and energy in the physical dimension. However, we had to recognize (although indirectly) that the Psi energy of the world of Pure Spirit which is made accessible by transcending the confrontation between subject and object, did create light in the light-proof room.

*b. Mechanism through Which Psi Energy Creates Light*

*i.* Was Psi Energy Converted Directly Into Light?

*ii.* In present-day physics, it is held that when atoms are excited by outside energy, the electrons which are on the ground-state orbits transit into the outer orbits and later return to their ground state. The excess energy, namely the energy quantum between the excited states and the ground states, is emitted as light waves. If this theory is applied to the above experiment, it can be considered that the Psi energy caused a transition of the outer-orbit electrons of certain atoms in the space of the shielded room (or certain atoms in the lower abdomen of the subject as light seemed to have been generated in that area), and thereby generated light in the shielded room. If so, should it be thought that the Psi energy directly made the electrons transit?

*iii.* In both *i.* and *ii.*, did the generation of light or the transition of electrons, resulting in emission of light, occur by way of some matter or energy system which intermediates Psi and physical energy?

At the moment, the mechanism for light generation through the function of Psi energy has not yet been clarified.

*c. Light Generated by Psi Energy Also Follows the Laws in the Physical Dimension*

As explained in the polygraph section, the lights which were recorded in segments (C) and (E) were not recorded by the video camera which was placed at a different angle from the photoelectric cell. This absence would be due to the difference between the field of view of the video camera and the diapason of the photoelectric cell (Figure 6). This fact suggests that the light which was generated by the function of Psi energy is also under the restrictions of time and space and follows physical laws.

*d. Control of Matter by the Mind*

As explained in the section on science, the observer's selection of the instrumentation influences the material phe-

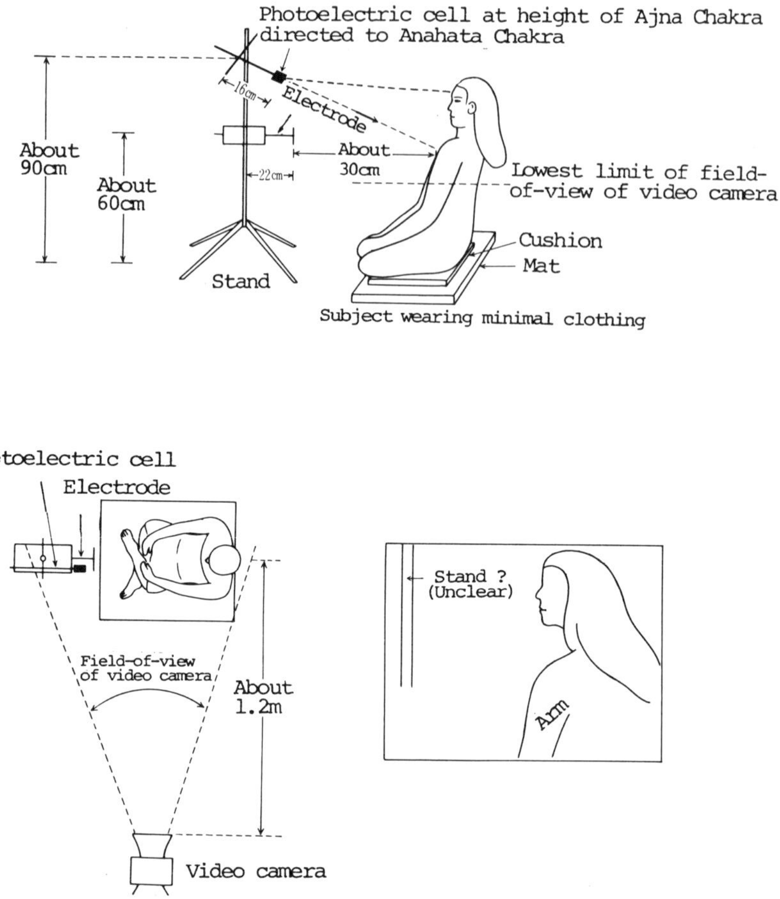


**Figure 6**: Location and Field-of-View of the Photoelectric Cell and Video Camera

nomena as object, and the nature of matter at the subatomic level is observed differently, depending on the instrumentation used.

When the influence of the observer's mind on material phenomena is compared with the influence of Pure Spirit through the function of Psi energy (in the dimension of subjective-objective oneness) there is a fundamental difference between the interaction of mind and matter in the scientific observation and that of the function of Psi energy.

In science it is not the mind itself, but physical energy (such as light functioning through the instrumentation selected by the mind) that influences the material phenomena as object. That is, it is not the interaction between mind and matter, but the interaction between matters. The observing mind itself does not influence the physical energy recorded by the instrumentation. In psychic phenomena, however, the Psi energy itself (which is mental energy) has an influence on the generation and extinction of material phenomena, although the mechanism of the influence is not yet known. The interaction between mind and matter in psychic phenomena is in fact the control of matter by the mind. Here is the fundamental and essential difference between the relation of observer and material phenomena on the subatomic level, and that of Pure Spirit and matter in the world of religion, where there is no confrontation between subject and object.

## D. The World of Religion Underlies the World of Science - *Towards the Unification of Science and Religion* -

As mentioned previously, in Psi phenomena, the mind itself is closely connected with the occurrence of material phenomena. This mind is Pure Spirit in the world of religion, where no confrontation between subject and object exists. The light which was surmised to have been generated by Psi energy (which belongs to the Pure Spirit) is a physical energy and functions under physical laws, and may thus be the object of scientific study.

From this line of thinking, the relationship between science and religion may be considered as follows : The Psi energy which belongs to the world of religion or Pure Spirit underlies the material world, which is the object of scientific study. It is this Psi energy which sustains material phenomena or the world of matter. Therefore it may be said that the world of religion underlies the world of science.

Viewed from the philosophical and ontological standpoint, mind and matter have their origin in the religious world (the world of Pure Spirit and the being as Topos) which is neither mind nor matter and where the subject and object are one. Thus the mind can observe matter as its object, interact with it, and thus establish science.

## E. Disappearance and Reappearance of A Paperweight - *The Conversion Between Mass and Energy* -

The following occurred in an experiment which had been conducted as preparation for the aforementioned light generation experiment.

During the experiment, one of the observers (Toshiaki Harada, Ph.D.) heard the noise of something small and hard falling on the floor in the shielded room. He heard another loud thud as if something bulky had fallen on the floor. He opened the door of the room and found that the subject M.Y. was lying on the floor in a faint. He also found a plastic paperweight on the floor in front of her. It was later discovered that this was one of my paperweights (plastic, cylindrical, 6.3 cm in diameter, 2 cm in height) which was kept in the second drawer of my desk in my room at the Institute. This is located on the second floor directly under the experiment room. The paperweight had penetrated the ceiling of the second floor and the floor of the third floor (made of copper, lead, and concrete) and fell on the floor of the shielded room with an audible noise.

How can we explain this phenomenon in connection with the observations of the light experiment? In modern subatomic physics, matter is a form of energy and is not solid and permanent in its nature. For example, the $\gamma$-ray extinguishes itself by generating an electron and a positron of equivalent mass. When the positron meets the electron, they extinguish themselves and create the $\gamma$-ray of energy equivalent to their mass. Matter is no more than a form of energy. A fluctuation of energy, or a "pack" of energy forms matter. What is it then that packs the energy?

To return to the paperweight, for the paperweight to pass through the concrete ceiling and wooden floor, it must be either extinguished or transformed into a type of physical energy which could penetrate the ceiling and floor, and then be reformed into its original form.

It would be possible for underlying Pure Spirit, which is beyond the discrimination of mind and matter, to extinguish the paperweight in the form of physical energy and to then recreate it. The subject M.Y. seems to have been in the same unified state with a 'universal power' as she was during the light experiment. It is difficult to grasp this world of religion within the framework of the world of science, however, because modern science is built upon the premise of the law of energy conservation. If the mechanism is elucidated on the interpretation that the Psi energy converted the paper weight from mass to energy and made it penetrate the ceiling and floor, and again converted it into paperweight form, this explanation would be accepted in science. From the above observations on the extinction and creation of the paperweight, it is my suggestion that that which packs the physical energy to form matter (the cause of formation in modern science) would be the Psi energy which belongs to the world of religion (where the subject and the object are one). It is also clear from the above disappearance and reappearance of the paperweight that this Psi energy converts matter into energy as well as forms the matter by converting the energy.

This phenomenon provides evidence that the world of religion underlies the material phenomena which are the objects of science. Capra says that the subatoms are not static particles of three-dimensional material, but are entities in the four-dimensional continuum of space-time, and that these entities are manifested as substance with mass in space and a process which contains energy equivalent to mass in time. The subatoms which are manifested in the four-dimensional continuum of space and time may well be a form of expression of Psi energy in the physical dimension.

Notes for Part II

1) *The World of Topos (Place)*: Kitaro Nishida (1870-1945), a foremost philosopher in modern Japan, used the word 'Topos' in his term 'logic of Topos'. Dr. Motoyama wrote in his book how and why he developed his idea of 'the world of Topos' as follows:

"I had been practicing Yoga for a few years before I had my first experience of the state of samadhi in which the mind and the object become as one, and at that time I came to a sudden realization that all is in the Self and the Self is in all. Some have described this revelation as 'cosmic consciousness', but I prefer the term 'Being as Topos'. I decided on this phrase when I recalled that Professor Nishida had used it in his books as a philosophical term during my university years, and I will explain why I believe that it is the most precise means of describing the experience of samadhi.

"The state of concentration involves both a self which concentrates and an object which is concentrated upon. When the practice of concentration is repeated and the mind extended in the astral dimension, this concentrating mind will gradually be integrated with the object and a partial union will occur. However, this limited union of subject and object is a long way from the experience in which the mind becomes totally one with the object.

"When the mind and the object are unified, the subject (the mind) becomes Topos, and the new unity is sustained and supported at its base. When the subject becomes Topos, this Topos can envelop within itself both the object which has stood apart and in opposition to the union and the mind (an inferior mind) which has maintained the differentiation. Unless the mind becomes fundamentally Topos, it cannot be united with the object, for if they are separate, they cannot be one.

"When the mind is superimposed on an object, they are not as one. Something must envelop and sustain the mind and the object before they can become one, and this 'something' must eradicate the base of their distinctiveness and must itself become the new integrity of subject and object. This basis of distinctiveness that exists in the material world prior to this oneness must be neutralized or temporarily suspended before the mind can merge with the object. Moreover, that which is temporarily neutralized becomes the 'something' which embraces the mind and the object and is their intrinsic coherence and support in the physical world. It follows that, if the mind and an object can become one, there must be a 'something' or a Topos which provides the transitional ground and becomes the new integrity by allowing the mind to leap into this 'Being as Topos' through the neutralization of the basis that gives rise to the distinction.

"When we think of God or the Absolute in these terms, it is clear that when He assumes His various forms as the Avalokitesvara bohisattva, the Buddha, and so on, we cannot equate the acts which He performs with his Being. The Absolute acts as It wills, and although we can talk about the acts of the 'Absolute', or refer to the agent by the name of 'God', the initiator of these acts is not the acts themselves. In worshipping 'God' or 'Buddha', man pays homage to only the facet or function of the Absolute. 'Being as Topos' designates the Absolute which is responsible for, but not synonymous with all things, and is consequently distinct from that which is ordinarily called 'God'." — Motoyama, H., *Towards a Superconsciousness : Meditational Theory and Practice*, pp81-84, Asian Humanities Press, (1990). (tr.)

2) *Being as Topos* : Please refer to the above. (tr.)

3) *Subject M.Y.* : For details on subject M.Y., please refer to Chapter II of Part I. (tr.)

4) *Her Male Friend* : In previous experiments, psychic phenomena had been more easily and often generated by M.Y. when

her male friend was with her and sent psychic power to her. We therefore asked him to be with her and cooperate in this experiment. (tr.)

5) *Pure Spirit* : Dr. Motoyama defined his understanding and term of 'Pure Spirit' in his proposed outline of the psychology course for the Masters and Ph.D. programs of his graduate school as follows:

"A Pure Spirit existence transcends the principles of matter and the law of karma and does not possess a body. The first step of liberation is attained here.

"By transcending the principles of matter, the Pure Spirit can now control and create the world of matter. Its prayers have a great influence on nature, space, mankind, and the earth.

"The human spirit that has reached the dimension of Pure Spirit transcends the world of karma and works to bring forth order and prosperity to a limited place, for example, a regional society, state, and the people who live in that society. The Pure Spirit supports all existence in that area. It is therefore called 'the Being as Topos' (animating and guiding force behind society). However, as long as the Pure Spirit is alive realistically the spirit also lives as an individual. This kind of individual is called the 'individual as Topos'. Its consciousness is pure superconsciousness, a type of universal consciousness."

In his psychology course, the subject of superconsciousness is also to be taught, together with unconsciousness and consciousness, including precise definitions of the difference between hypnosis and religious experience. Details of the graduate school can be obtained from :

The Institute for Religious Psychology
(President: Hiroshi Motoyama, Ph.D., Ph.D.)
4-11-7 Inokashira, Mitaka-shi, Tokyo 181, Japan
Tel : (0422) 48-3535 Fax : (0422) 48-3548 (tr.)

# References

1. Avalon, A., *The Serpent Power*, Ganeth & Co. Ltd., India, 1953.

2. Grof, S., Capra F., et al., *Ancient Wisdom and Modern Science*, edited by S. Grof, State University of New York Press, New York, 1984.

3. Ingram, J.E., *Radiation and Quantum Physics*, Oxford University Press, 1973.

4. Kosoto, J., et al., *Ishaku Kotei Daikei Reisu*, (Interpretation of the Yellow Emperor's Classic of Internal Medicine, Ling Shu), Chikuji Shoten, Tokyo, 1974.

5. Kosoto, J., et al., *Ishaku Kotei Daikei Somon*, (Interpretation of the Yellow Emperor's Classic of Internal Medicine, Su Wen), Chikuji Shoten, Tokyo, 1974.

6. Kosoto, J., et al., *Ishaku Hachijuichi Nangyo*, (Interpretation of Nei Ching), Chikuji Shoten, Tokyo, 1974.

7. Leadbeater, C.W., *The Chakras*, The Theospohical Publishing House, India, 1969.

8. Motoyama, H., *Theories of the Chakras*, Theosophical Publishing House, Wheaton, Illinois, 1981.

9. Motoyama, H., *Science and the Evolution of Consciousness*, Autumn Press, Massachusetts, 1978.

10. Motoyama, *H., How to Measure and Diagnose the Function of the Meridians and Their Corresponding Internal Organs,* the Institute for Religious Psychology, Tokyo, 1975.

11. Motoyama, H., "Electrophysiological and Preliminary Biochemical Studies of Skin Properties in Relation to the Acupuncture Meridian", *Research for Religion and Parapsychology*, June 1980, pp. 1-37.

12. Motoyama, H., "A Biophysical Elucidation of the Meridian and Ki Energy", *Research for Religion and Parapsychology*,

August 1981.

13. Motoyama, H., *Shukyo no Shinka to Kagaku*, (The Evolution of Religion and Science), Shukyo Shinri Shuppan, Tokyo, 1982.

14. Motoyama, H., "PK Influence on the Meridians and Psi-Energy", *Research for Religion and Parapsychology*, July 1979.

15. Motoyama, H., *Toyo Igaku: Ki no Nagare no Sokutei, Shindan to Chiryo*, (Oriental Medicine: Measurement, Diagnosis and Treatment of Ki), Shukyo Shinri Shuppan, Tokyo, 1985.

16. Nakane, G. et al. (tr.), *Upanishad Zensho*, (Compendium of the Upanishads), Sekaibunko Kankokai, Tokyo, 1923.

17. T. Sahota, *Kaisetsu Yoga Sutra*, (An Interpretation of Yoga Sutra), Kobunsha, Tokyo, 1966.

18. Satyananda, S., *Asana, Pranayama, Mudra, Bandha*, Bihar School of Yoga, India, 1969.

19. Satyananda, S., *Tantra of Kundalini Yoga*, Bihar School of Yoga, India, 1973.

20. Shirota, F., *Shinkyu Chiryo Kisogaku*, (Basics of Acupuncture Treatment), Ido-no-Nippon-sha, Tokyo, 1931.

21. Shirota, F., *Shinkyu Chiryo no Jissai*, (Clinical Cases of Acupuncture Treatment), Ido-no-Nippon-Sha, Tokyo, 1967.

22. Tomonaga, S., *Butsurigaku Dokuhon*, (A Reading of Physics), Misuzu Shobo, Tokyo, 1969.

# PROFILE OF THE AUTHOR

Dr. Hiroshi Motoyama, a well-known Japanese scholar, was born in 1925 in Japan. Dr. Motoyama graduated from the Tokyo University of Literature and Science with Ph.D. degrees in philosophy and physiological psychology, and was awarded a prestigious prize for his work in the comparative study of Eastern and Western mysticism.

Dr. Motoyama is both a scientist trained in empirical methodology, and a psychic who has experientially gained deep philosophical knowledge. He is the head Shinto priest of the Tamamitsu Shrine in Tokyo, and a yogi well-versed in the yoga treatises.

**Establishments, Publications and Academic Activities**

His scientific endeavors resulted in the establishment of the Institute for Religious Psychology, a research facility (1960), and the International Association for Religion and Parapsychology, an international organization whose members are not only composed of scientists in these and related fields, but are from diverse professions (1972). For specialized research in the field of life physics, the Motoyama Institute for Life Physics was established in 1990.

Dr. Motoyama is the author of over 50 books (Japanese

and other languages) and numerous monographs and papers. He has traveled widely throughout the world, participating and presenting his work in conferences and workshops. (The details of his books/monographs in English and academic activities are listed separately.)

### Awards

In recognition of his important work in the field, he was awarded the McDougall Research Fund Award from Duke University, U.S.A., in 1962; selected as one of the world's leading parapsychologists by UNESCO in 1974; and recognized as an ordinary academician by the Instituto di Cultura Universitaria e di Studi Superiori, Academia Tiberina, Italy, in 1977. He has also been honored by several renowned scientific and religious organizations. He serves as an advisor/lecturer to various international associations and institutes and as a member of the editorial board of international magazines in related fields.

### Devices and Research Findings

In the course of his scientific research he devised two instruments: the AMI (the Apparatus for measuring the functioning of the Meridians and their corresponding Internal organs), which monitors the flow of Ki and meridian functioning; and the Chakra Instrument, which monitors the bio-energy fields surrounding the body.

Through research with the AMI, he verified that:

1) There is a current which flows in the dermis and epidermis before the formation of polarization generated against the externally applied stimulation, and this before polarization(BP) current flows primarily in the water-rich phase of the dermal connective tissue;
2) Ki energy flow or the meridian system is a different energy system that actually exists apart from the nervous system, and the before polarization(BP) current is a parameter reflecting the meridian functioning;
3) The water-rich phase of the dermal and other connective

tissue is the physical formation of the acupuncture meridian and is the reservoir of Ki;

4) The four parameters of the monitored AMI wave form indicate;
   a ) Before polarization(BP) value is the parameter of the functioning of the meridian and Ki system,
   b ) After polarization(AP) value is the parameter of the functioning of the autonomic nervous system,
   c ) Total electrical charge mobilized for polarization(IQ) is the parameter of the metabolism and homeostatic function,
   d ) Time to complete the polarization (TC) is the parameter of the velocity of the body's reaction against the given stimulation.

(The details should be found in note 1) of Chapter Ⅱ.)

Through research using the Chakra Instrument and other physiological measurements, Dr. Motoyama verified that the Psi or mental energy and its energy centers (so-called Chakras) actually exist. He shed scientific light on the mechanism of the generation of the physical phenomena and on the mechanism of the conversion between physiological (physical) energy and psychological (mental) energy, as well.

For the first time in history, Dr. Motoyama bridged the Indian Chakra-Nadi system and the Chinese meridian system, and discovered that there is a close connection between the physical constitution (meridian functioning) and psychic abilities (Chakra awakening). On the basis of the aforementioned research findings and his own experience of the higher state of consciousness, he proposes Energy Medicine as a future form of preventive medicine.

**For Research Cooperation and for Students**

In 1980, he established the Motoyama-Bentov Fund Research Fellowship to assist promising scientists who wish to study human existence in its holistic sense, as well as continuing his own academic career.

In 1991, he established the Southern California Institute Japan Branch (Graduate School) in Tokyo, and is now the president. He plans to expand this graduate school as CIHS (California Institute for Human Science) with an international perspective in the near future, in the hopes of :

1) Elucidating the mechanism of the correlation between mind and body,
2) Understanding the human mind (unconscious, conscious, superconscious),
3) Synthesizing Eastern and Western religions,
4) Synthesizing Eastern and Western medicine (energy medicine and health science).

He wishes to invite reputable researchers and scholars as professors of the school in order to train young and talented researchers. Dr. Motoyama has taken steps for realizing the establishment of CIHS on the belief that this project is important for the realization of a global society - one which will require individuals with mental and spiritual maturity.

Readers who wish to learn more about Dr. Motoyama's work, and those who share his interest in the scientific research of Psi phenomena and the study of religious experience, may contact the Institute for Religious Psychology or the Motoyama Institute for Life Physics at the following address:

4-11-7 Inokashira, Mitaka-shi,
Tokyo 181, Japan
Tel: (0422) 48-3535
Fax: (0422) 48-3548

# ACADEMIC ACTIVITIES OF DR. MOTOYAMA

| | | |
|---|---|---|
| 1962 | U.S.A. | Researcher and lecturer at Duke University |
| 1963 | India | Researcher and lecturer at Rajasthan University |
| 1964 | England | Lecturer at the First International Parapsychological Conference |
| 1967 | Japan | Lecturer at the International Congress of Psychosomatic Medicine |
| 1969 | India | Visiting professor at Andhra University |
| 1972 | U.S.A. | Lecturer at the Convention of the ESP Foundation |
| 1972 | Japan | Chairman, Psychophysiology section at the International Congress for Psychology |
| 1974 | U.S.A. | Guest lecturer at Stanford University, the Sky Foundation, and Miami Heart Institute |
| 1975 | Korea | Lecturer at the First World Congress of Manipulation Therapy |
| | U.S.A. | Guest lecturer at the Miami Heart Institute |
| | Italy | Lecturer at the International Congress on Parapsychology |
| 1976 | U.S.A. | Lecturer at the Fifth International Conference on the Unity of the Sciences |
| | Spain | Vice-chairman and lecturer at the First World Congress of Parapsychology |
| | Mexico | Lecturer at First International Congress of Paranormal Phenomena |
| | Japan | Guest lecturer at the Third International Congress on Psychotronic Research |

| | | |
|---|---|---|
| | Swiss | Lecturer at the Swiss Association for Acupuncture |
| 1978 | U.S.A. | Presented workshop at California Institute of Integral Studies |
| | U.S.A. | Lecturer at the Third International Congress of Yoga, Meditation and Holistic Health |
| | U.S.A. | Guest lecturer at the Miami Heart Institute and Emory University, Atlanta |
| | Canada | Lecturer at Spiritual Science Fellowship, and Montreal Center for the Healing Arts |
| 1979 | Brazil | Presented a paper at the Fourth International Congress on Psychotronic Research |
| 1981 | U.S.A. | Guest lecturer at the Conference, Healing in Our Time |
| 1982 | India | Lecturer at Mahatma Gandhi Medical College |
| | U.S.A. | Guest lecturer at The School of Spiritual Healing |
| 1984 | Japan | Lecturer at the Japan-France International Symposium |
| 1985 | Japan | Lecturer at the Japan Society of Acupuncture |
| 1986 | Japan | Guest lecturer at the Japan Herbal Medicine Association |
| 1987 | Japan | Presented co-authored paper at the International College of Craniomandibular Orthopedics |
| 1988 | Japan | Guest lecturer at the Japan Society of Autonomous Nervous System |
| | Japan | Guest lecturer at the Japan Dental Society of Oriental Medicine |

| | | |
|---|---|---|
| | Brasil | Guest lecturer at the Second International Congress on Alternative Therapies |
| 1989 | U.S.A. | Guest lecturer at Oakland University, School of Health Sciences |
| | U.S.A. | Guest lecturer at the Energy Fields, Meridians, Ki and Device Technology Roundtable organized by the Fetzer Foundation |
| 1990 | England | Guest lecturer at Exeter University |
| | Holland | Guest lecturer at the New Momentum Health Care Centre |
| | France | Lecturer at the First International Congress on the Energy Body of Man |
| | U.S.A. | Lecturer at Hawaii University |
| | Japan | Lecturer at Sophia University |
| 1991 | U.S.A. | Lecturer at the San Francisco State University |
| | U.S.A. | Lecturer at the California Institute for Integral Studies |
| | Japan | Lecturer at the Tokyo Dental Research Society |
| | Japan | Lecturer at the Nichiren Institute for Modern Religions |

# PUBLICATIONS

**Books by Dr. Hiroshi Motoyama**

*Science and the Evolution of Consciousness - Chakras, Ki and Psi -* (1978). ISBN : 0-394-73634-6. Published by Autumn Press, U.S.A.

*Theories of the Chakras - Bridge to Higher Consciousness* (1981). ISBN : 0-8356-0551-5. Published by the Theosophical Publishing House, U.S.A.

*Towards a Superconsciousness - Meditational Theory and Practice -* (1990). ISBN : 0-89581-914-7. Published by Asian Humanities Press, U.S.A.

*How to Measure and Diagnose the Functions of the Merid-ians and Their Corresponding Internal Organs* (1975). Published by the Institute for Religious Psychology, Japan

*Hypnosis and Religious Superconsciousness* (1971). Published by the Institute for Religious Psychology, Japan

**I.R.P. Monographs**

The Present Situation of Parapsychology in the World (1969)

Psychic Surgery in the Philippines (1972)

Chakra, Nadi of Yoga, and the Meridian Points of Acupuncture (1972)

The Non-Physical in the Correlation Between Mind and Body (1972)

The Mechanism through Which Paranormal Phenomena Take Place (1975)

The Ejection of Energy from the Chakra of Yoga and Meridian Points of Acupuncture (1975)

A Psychophysiological Study of Yoga (1976)

Tony Agpaoa's Psychic Surgery and Its Mechanism (1978)

**I.A.R.P. Journals :** ***Research for Religion and Parapsychology***

Do Meridians Exist and What Are They Like? (1975)
(Out of print)

How to Measure and Diagnose the Functions of Meridians (1975)
(Out of print)

Realization of a Religious World (Out of print) (1976)

Religion and Parapsychology (Proceedings of the 5th Annual Convention of the IARP) (1976)

Hypnosis, Psychosis, Religious Experience (Out of print) (1976)

Western and Eastern Medical Studies of Pranayama and Heart Control (1977)

An Electrophysiological Study of Prana (Ki) (1978)

Yoga and Oriental Medicine (1979)

PK Influence on the Meridians and Psi Energy (1979)

The Realization of Holistic Health and Its Science (Proceedings of the 8th Annual Convention of the IARP) (1979)

Das Mystische Erlebnis und das "Absolute Nichts" der Gott,der Geist und die Natur (1950)

Electrophysiological and Preliminary Biochemical Studies of Skin Properties in Relation to the Acupuncture Meridian; A Scientific Study of Religion (Under revision) (1980)

A Biophysical Elucidation of the Meridian and Ki Energy (1981)

Self-Training for Psychic Development - Part I (1981)
(Under revision)

The Meridian Exercises (Under revision) (1982)

Self-Training for Psychic Development - Part II (1983)
(Under revision)

Karma and Reincarnation (Proceedings of the 11th Annual Convention of the IARP) (1984)

Function of Ki and Psi Energy - with Special Reference to Experiments on the Toate (Distant Hitting) of Shintaido (a Japanese Martial Art) (1985)

Meridians and Ki - Measurements, Diagnoses and Treatment Principles with the AMI (1986)

Psychophysiological Changes Due to the Performance of the Phowa Ritual; Analyses of Real Cases of Near-Death Experiences (1987)

Guidelines for Awakening the Chakras (1988)

Worlds after Death -I- (Proceedings of the 12th Annual Convention of the IARP) (1989)

Available from:
Human Science Press (Shukyo Shinri Shuppan)
4-11-7 Inokashira, Mitaka-shi, Tokyo 181,
Japan
Tel: (0422) 48-3535
Fax: (0422) 48-3548

# INDEX

## S



## T



## V



## Y

# AFTERWARD

Dr. Hiroshi Motoyama is a sage in the age of science. Combining the ancient wisdom with the recent developments in science and technology, Dr. Motoyama has made it his life's mission to take science to religion and religion to science. He is convinced that there is no conflict between the best in the scientific and religious traditions. The work in the area of parapsychology bears testimony to the unity of knowledge and shows the points where there is a confluence between religious thought and scientific findings.

Dr. Motoyama is uniquely qualified to undertake this gigantic task of seeking the unification of religion and science. A practicing Shinto Priest, he is well-trained in philosophy and psychology and has extensive familiarity with Eastern esoteric traditions such as Indian yoga and Chinese Ki. Having collaborated with Dr. J.B. Rhine, Dr. Motoyama is exposed to the best of the parapsychological tradition as well. Even more unusual is his gift for invention as evidenced by the ingenious instrumentation such as the AMI and the Chakra machine he developed which in addition to being extremely useful for his research seem to hold promise as valuable diagnostic tools in health care.

Dr. Motoyama's work has important implications for

developing suitable research methods for exploring the subjective phenomena through empirical methods. His approach, it seems to me, is an example of subjective empiricism of the kind Buddha had expounded. Science postulates a basic dichotomy between the subject (known) and the object (unknown) and attempts to study the latter by excluding the former. Religious experience at its best transcends this dichotomy and results in a state of consciousness where they merge in a oneness, giving us a glimpse of reality far more profound than what our ordinary experience can give us. The physical constraints on our consciousness, including the barriers of space and time that are themselves a consequence of the subject/object dichotomy built into the scientific discourse, disappear for example in meditation. Dr. Motoyama's research findings are more than the laboriously collected data that he and his colleagues have accumulated over the years, they also reflect his deep convictions and personal experiences born out of prolonged and persistent practice of the disciplines he advocates.

In the present book Dr. Motoyama sets out first to introduce yogic discipline and Chinese Meridian-Ki system in their relation to health and healing. He then goes on to present the data he had collected based on these concepts. In the second part of the book, which is probably the more important part, he explores the unity of science and religion through the medium of Psi energy which he believes is evidenced by the experimental results. According to Dr. Motoyama mind in its superconscious state does not merely influence matter. Rather it can create or destroy matter. Conscious control of natural phenomena, he points out, "provides evidence that spiritual evolution into a higher being" is possible. Psi energy, according to Dr. Motoyama, is "mental energy which belongs to the Pure Spirit in a higher dimension of being. So it is beyond the restrictions of matter in time and space. The physical walls of the shielded room are no obstacle in such a world of being." It is the confrontation between the subject and the object that underlies all science and distinguishes scientifc knowledge from the transcendental experience of the Pure Spirit where there is no such dichotomy.

Whatever may be the final scientific verdict on Dr. Motoyama's experiments and his conclusions, he will be respected for his scholarship and admired for his courage and innovative approach. He stands alone today as a pioneer in this attempted synthesis of science and religion, Eastern thought and Western Science and technology. I am convinced more than ever that Dr. Motoyama's ideas deserve greater attention and consideration than they have received so far.

If this book could interest at least a few scientists to closely study Dr. Motoyama's work, replicate his experiments and develop on his instruments, it would have served a very useful purpose.

K. Ramakrishna Rao, Ph.D.,
Director, Foundation for Research
on the Nature of Man,
North Carolina, U.S.A.